Praise for A 'Grocery' Christmas Carol

"Everyone thinks they know all about their favorite grocery store, but do they? Scott Moses guides you through supermarkets' start, their current state and where this century's old industry is going. While grocery geeks like me will really enjoy this read, so too will anyone else who shops for groceries."

-Jim Donald – Chairman and Former CEO, Albertsons; Former CEO, Starbucks, Extended Stay America, Haggen and Pathmark

"An amazing collection of data that demonstrates the current and unquestioned future of the neighborhood grocery store. It is a shame this fabric of the community could be a thing of the past. Not today, or tomorrow, but we are on that course. Well done."

-Mike Schlotman – Former CFO, Kroger

"Scott's book is one of the best industry overviews I've ever read. Once I started reading it, I couldn't stop. Scott hits the nail on the head with his insights and wealth of industry knowledge. He's in the engine room and gives the reader a glimpse of how food retailing has, and is, changing. It's dynamic. I'm buying this book for our management team and, especially, the next generation of family leadership at Stew Leonard's!"

-Stew Leonard, Jr. – Chairman and CEO, Stew's Leonard's

"Scott Moses is the expert on the competitive state of American grocery. As an investment banker, he is the leading advisor in the grocery industry. His analysis of the evolution of the industry is a must-read for its insights."

-Peter J. Solomon – Chairman, Solomon Partners

"A compelling narrative that captures much of the modern history of our industry. This should become the grocery textbook of our time, and in my view, should be required reading for grocers, CPG companies and economics majors across the country."

"Evolution is constant in retail, but nowhere is it felt more personally than in our local supermarkets. The stores that have served our families for decades are under siege from a new range of well-armed and well-capitalized offerings. Scott masterfully analyzes the industry's competitive shifts and paints a sobering picture of the potential future of the supermarket if incumbents are left to fend for themselves. This book is a compelling read for anyone interested in the industry."

"This fast-paced, fact-based supermarket business read has everything you need to know about U.S. grocery past, present and future, factually told by the guru of our industry. Moses has scripted a loud industry wake-up call heralding the necessity for continued grocery mergers and acquisitions. Brilliantly bolstered with informative graphs and charts (putting strategy development and data driven decision-making at your fingertips), Moses masterfully augments these facts by interweaving a sincere personal homage to the leaders and legions of workers who have shaped the grocery landscape over the past 20 years, leaving no doubt they are the lead story in his heart and mind."

"As a grocery retailer that has been serving communities for nearly 100 years, we've witnessed incredible transformations in our industry over the years. This book captures how evolving consumer habits and increasingly intense competition have driven the expansion into diverse retail formats. It's a great resource for understanding the shifts we've seen and inspiring a forward-thinking approach for the future of food retail. I appreciate Scott's friendship and the valuable knowledge he has shared over the years."

-Brad Brookshire – Chairman and CEO, Brookshire Grocery Co.

"Great read! It's like packing 20+ years of strategic conversations I've had with Scott all into one book. The impact of the Walmart tsunami in the late 1990s/2000s continues, while new waves build. Scott captures it all."

Rob Woseth – Former CFO, Supervalu

"Scott Moses, as demonstrated by his career success and depth of character, has captured the essence of a unique situation and its long-range implications on the industry and the economy."

-Alice Elliot – Founder, CEO, The Elliot Group

"Scott's work sounds a crucial alarm on the risk of our trusted supermarkets slipping away to discount retailers, with serious consequences for our communities. He highlights how these stores are more than places to shop; they are vital to local jobs, community ties and access to quality food. His message reminds us of the urgent need to protect these essential hubs before it's too late."

-Sylvain Perrier – President of North America & COO, Mercatus

"Scott provides a deep understanding and historical view to the evolution of grocery and a glimpse of the future. He does an amazing job reminding us how critical supermarket grocers are to everyone."

-Tom O'Boyle – Former COO, Family Dollar;
Former CEO, Marsh Supermarkets

"Scott Moses is not just one of the most astute observers of the supermarket industry, he's also someone who has been intimately involved in many of the financial deals that have reshaped the industry, reset the competitive balance and created a business better able to serve customers. And, he is one of the industry's most passionate defenders. This book combines all these attributes into a compelling narrative, explaining to insiders and outsiders alike the cold realities of industry workings, how the business has evolved to this place and time, and, most importantly in my view, what the future might – and should – hold."

-Kevin Coupe – "Content Guy," MorningNewsBeat.com

A 'Grocery' Christmas Carol:
The Ghost of Supermarkets Future

Perspectives from a Leading Mergers Advisor
on an Industry Under Siege

SCOTT MOSES

For Jessica and Gabi, who are all my reasons.

Table of Contents

Foreword

In March 2020, as New York City was locking down and Covid fear was gripping the world, my family and I began what would become ten weeks of "shelter in place." We did not leave our apartment building for ten weeks. That's *70 days*.

Sirens all day and night; mobile morgues all around the city. It was scary, and it was surreal. Here's the view down Third Avenue from the roof of my apartment building in April 2020, a month into the lockdown, in the middle of the day. Streets that were usually packed with bumper-to-bumper traffic were empty, with barely a moving vehicle in sight.

I was one of those people you might remember seeing on the news that spring, cheering from our windows at 7 p.m. each night to honor healthcare workers

1

and resolutely rally the spirit of "the city that never sleeps" even as we saw 'the lights go out on Broadway' and countless other hellish tribulations.

<u>Ask yourself</u>: *How would you have fed your family that spring without your local grocers?*

I've lived in Manhattan for over 25 years. I don't know about you, but I'm not much of a farmer. I'm not much of a hunter or gardener. I'm not sure how we would have survived that period were it not for the extraordinary American grocery industry, which has sustained us all during crisis after crisis across the country — hurricanes, tornadoes and now, a pandemic.

There's no overstating it: **Our grocery industry *really matters*.**

Fortunately, during Covid, we were able to receive a steady stream of groceries from four different online grocers. Like millions of other new amateur chefs, we learned to cook a bunch of great recipes at home that we never previously considered, including homemade pizza that was objectively spectacular (being a New Yorker, I can opine on this with some measure of authority).

As a mergers and acquisitions advisor to the grocery industry, I was working at the time (with my team) with various grocers around the country whose senior executives regularly shared the challenges, fears and exigencies related to keeping their teams and their customers safe.

I often reflect on those early Covid years of incalculable hardship and sacrifice, endured in a Dantesque inferno. In the United States alone, we lost over one million loved ones too soon, including one of my favorite people in the world, my great aunt, Sylvia Scheer.

One morning in March 2020, as it was becoming clear that life as we knew it was being suspended, I woke up with a series of deep emotions flooding through me. I sat down at my desk and just started typing. A few minutes later, I was staring at this message of hope, which I then shared with thousands of friends around the industry:

An Open Thank You Note

March 20, 2020

To My Friends Across the Grocery Industry:
Thank You — We Are With You.

As a customer and a citizen, I want to thank each of you and your teams for the heroic work you are doing to help sustain all of us and our families during this difficult time.

I often talk about supermarkets being the families who feed America's families and the important role your stores have played as pillars of thousands of American communities — for generations — not just for customers, but for the millions of teammates working in stores.

In a crisis, this is exponentially more apparent; grocers consistently are the last ones to leave and the first ones back in.

The pivotal role our industry is playing during this extraordinary time is truly inspiring. I believe the way you are rising to this challenge to serve your communities during this time is going to be remembered for a long time to come, indelibly branding the hearts of your customers with lifetime loyalty...

On a personal level, I have never been more proud to be associated with this industry.

I wish all of you and your families good health and the fortitude you will need to continue the Herculean work ahead of you.

We are all pulling for you and know you will meet the challenge, with grit and grace.

With extreme gratitude,
Scott Moses

Re-reading these words, I'm reminded of the remarkable way our millions of indomitable, essential grocery teammates across the country answered the bell each day to resiliently rise above a seemingly never-ending series of unpredictable hurdles and help feed hundreds of millions of Americans 21 meals per week (that's billions of meals, each week). They truly are pillars of thousands of American communities, as they have been for generations.

I hope you take away the same flood of pride in our ability to take care of each other, and particularly an appreciation of our irreplaceable American grocery family — committed to health, safety, science and common sense — setting a stoic example that should encourage everyone to be the best version of themselves. It inspires me to remain defiantly optimistic about what we can achieve if we focus on the many things that unite us rather than those that tear us apart.

Covid starkly reinforced my deep love and gratitude for American grocery — particularly our supermarket grocers and their teammates — and helped catalyze a crusade of articles, speeches, TV appearances, press briefings and other presentations (many before the Kroger/Albertsons merger, and many working for Albertsons over the past two years in support of it) which have become this book.

It is designed to equip industry leaders, observers and the public with a dashboard of facts with which to properly evaluate what's happening to the supermarket grocers in our industry and the intensifying, existential risks they face. I hope you find it helpful and join me in my quest to protect them.

Scott Moses
Summer 2024

Introduction

One of the most consequential books I read as a boy was *A Christmas Carol* by Charles Dickens. During Covid, I was inspired to re-read the book. As many readers know, the classic story revolves around the life — and potential demise — of Ebenezer Scrooge, a mean, miserly countinghouse owner who only learns to appreciate the error of his ways when he is reminded of the past, sees the present from another angle and is given a horrifying glimpse into his future were he not to make amends. In this fictional world, Scrooge gets the opportunity to pivot, change his life and enhance not only his own future, but that of the good people around him, many of whom rely on him. There is bona fide wisdom in this story.

In a brilliant exposition of supermarkets past (though part of "Christmas present" in the 1843 book), Dickens demonstrates the wonder and delight of London's grocers and the Christmas bounty they offered:

> *The Grocers! Oh the Grocers!...the blended scents of tea and coffee...so grateful to the nose...raisins so plentiful and rare...almonds so extremely white...sticks of cinnamon so long and straight...other spices so delicious...candied fruits so caked and spotted with molten sugar as to make the coldest lookers-on feel faint and subsequently bilious...[T]he Grocer and his people were so frank and fresh that the polished hearts with which they fastened their aprons behind might have been their own, worn outside for general inspection...*

Millions of teammates in the grocery community have experienced that magnificent feeling in their stores over their years of customer engagement. Many thankfully still get to experience it today. The question is how long that can continue.

* * *

I fell in love with the grocery industry during my first client engagement as a young banker over 20 years ago. I was working on debt financing for Pathmark, which coincidentally was my family's local grocer when I was a boy growing up on Long Island. Pathmark had a store about a mile away from our home, in the shopping center right near my elementary school.

Our assignment was to help Pathmark's senior management team sell bonds as part of a refinancing of their capital structure. In order to do that, we had to prepare a presentation that the company's CEO, CFO and SVP of Real Estate would deliver several dozen times on a roadshow, over several weeks, to potential debt investors all around the country.

This was nearly 20 years before Zoom video calls, so we had to charter a plane to take us to a bunch of cities, sometimes three or four in one day. My role was to work with senior management to prepare the roadshow presentation, assist in prep sessions, facilitate the logistics of the trip and help the team do their best as they engaged with potential investors.

Here's the important part: Pathmark's CEO was Jim Donald, one of the lions of American grocery; CFO Frank Vitrano and SVP of Real Estate Harvey Gutman were also among the very best in the industry.

Jim Donald started his career as a teenager in Florida at Publix and then Albertsons, where he met his mentor, another lion of the industry, Bob Miller. After various roles with Albertsons, Jim went to Walmart and helped Sam Walton develop the Walmart Supercenter. He later ran Safeway's Eastern

Division and then became CEO of Pathmark. Jim subsequently went on to become CEO of Starbucks, Haggen, Extended Stay Hotels and Albertsons (where he is Chairman of the Board).

Frank Vitrano had been at Pathmark nearly 30 years at the time and subsequently was CFO of Rite Aid, guiding that company through some significant challenges. Since retiring, Frank now sits on the board of Northeast Grocery, the product of the merger we arranged between Price Chopper and Tops in upstate New York that closed in 2021 (after a courtship that took several years). Harvey Gutman has been a leader in grocery real estate for over 30 years.

So much of professional success comes down to luck; endless hard work is necessary, but even being on the right team is simply not sufficient.

To prepare for the roadshow presentations, I got to visit the company in New Jersey and see the team in action at their headquarters in Carteret. Once the roadshow started, I got to sit in on 60 or 70 meetings, intently listening and learning as Jim, Frank and Harvey talked about the industry and different facets of the company. When we visited stores, I got to see how real leaders mobilize and motivate their team to serve customers at the highest level, every day. I write "got to" because it was an incredible privilege to even *meet* these exceptional people, let alone spend so much time with them.

I could not have been more fortunate than to get years-worth of education in a few weeks as I watched these extraordinary leaders engage with their team and educate investors about the grocery industry. The warm, welcoming ethos of American grocery was palpable in every meeting — ***it was family, at work.*** It was eye-opening and instructive for a recent graduate who knew next to nothing about a real industry in the real world. I was hooked, and I've never looked back.

Ever since that first project with Pathmark, I've been advising grocers on mergers and acquisitions, primarily sales. We have helped dozens of clients, mostly family businesses, execute transactions that have saved or strengthened thousands of stores and hundreds of thousands of jobs. It has been a deep honor at which, in complete humility, I still marvel every time I think about it.

But it all started with Jim, Frank and Harvey: dozens of meetings; nearly as many hands of a card game they taught me called Red Dog (on the plane and in the car between meetings — for money — which was a no-win situation for me, the kid of the group); and a few memorable games of "conference room H-O-R-S-E" just before some investor meetings started. (Yes, we played basketball in huge investors' fancy conference rooms. All we needed was a paper ball, a trash can and some good creative shots.) It was one of the greatest experiences of my life.

That was my introduction to this unique and incomparable industry. Little did I know at the time how necessary — and how vulnerable — it is.

CHAPTER 1

The Ghost of Supermarkets Past

American grocery has evolved extensively over the past 100 years. At the start of the 20th century, customers would go to a general store, where a clerk would gather for them the items they requested. It was fairly inefficient, requiring the clerk to do all of the store procurement labor. This extremely high labor cost limited the inventory a grocer could afford to offer, so the shopping experience in the store was not terribly exciting.

King Kullen in New York and Piggly Wiggly in Memphis, among others, changed all this in the early 1900s by opening up the store and enabling customers to pick their own items, thereby transferring a significant amount of in-store labor from the grocer to the customer. The incremental efficiency enabled the grocer to offer more inventory; buying more inventory at scale lowered cost per unit; lowering costs per unit led to lower prices, which attracted customers to buy more products. Over time, the rise of supermarkets transformed American grocery.

In the past hundred years, there have been numerous variations on the grocery model, from the smaller-box, no-frills discount grocery stores that Aldi and Lidl developed in post-war Germany, to the hypermarkets created by Carrefour in Europe that inspired Sam Walton to develop Walmart Supercenters, to club grocers built by Price Club and Costco (and Walton again, with Sam's Club), to online grocery platforms like Amazon, Instacart and Shipt (now owned by Target). Numerous books have been written about this evolution, so I will not cover it in much detail here.

For our purposes, what matters is the undeniable reality that American grocery has expanded to include many formats, and consumer shopping habits have evolved with the formats offered to them. As consumer habits evolved, the competitive dynamics for supermarket grocers, which have always had very thin margins, got very intense. Prices came down, and margins and cash flow came down with them.

The Decline of a Southern Institution

Winn-Dixie's roots go back to a general store in Idaho founded by William Davis and his four sons in 1914. Most of the store's sales were on credit. As quasi-supermarkets began to transform grocery, a new chain called Skaggs Cash Store (a predecessor of Albertsons and Safeway) required cash-only purchases. This less-risky model allowed Skagg's to lower prices on food while widening selection.[1] In an eerie parallel to the experience of so many supermarket grocers in recent years, the combination of a recession in 1921 and continued competition from a strong entrant in Skagg's destabilized the Davis family's business. It eventually closed.

Davis moved to Miami in 1925, borrowed $10,000 from his father and bought a grocery store that become the foundation for a series of acquisitions, including Winn & Lovett and Dixie Home, which formed the basis for its new name in 1955. Even though Winn-Dixie went public in the 1950s, the Davis family always controlled the company.

In 1981, Sam Walton joined the board of directors of Winn-Dixie. Walton served on the Winn-Dixie board until 1986. Soon after that, Walmart opened

---

[1] https://floridahistoryblog.com/winn-dixie-and-davis-family/

its first Walmart Supercenter. The next year, Winn-Dixie reached its peak, with roughly 1,300 stores across the southern U.S., including locations as far west as Texas and Oklahoma, and as far north as Ohio and Indiana. That was the beginning of a long, steep decline.

At that time, in the late 1980s, supermarket grocers comprised the overwhelming majority of grocery sales in the United States. That was about to change. In the following two decades, Walmart blanketed the Southeast with supercenters, transforming the regional grocery market and undermining Winn-Dixie as much as any other grocer.

In 2005, after several years of declining sales, Winn-Dixie filed for bankruptcy protection. The company announced it would close or sell 326 locations (35 percent of its total) and roughly 22,000 teammates (28 percent of its total) would lose their jobs. The reorganization plan called for the rationalization of all Winn-Dixie stores in North Carolina, South Carolina, Tennessee and Virginia, as well as exits from parts of Georgia, Alabama, Mississippi and Louisiana.[2]

The causes were very clear to the Federal Reserve of Richmond, which wrote in an article at the time: "Traditionally, profit margins of supermarkets are thin. Competition from mass merchandisers like Wal-Mart and Target and drugstore chains like CVS and Walgreens has squeezed margins further."[3]

After nearly 90 years, the Davis family was no longer in the grocery business.

It was a precursor for supermarket grocers across the United States, as this story has repeated itself numerous times in various regions of the country. Longstanding incumbents have been overrun by secular changes in the industry and a series of new competitors, particularly Walmart.

---

[2] https://www.supermarketnews.com/archive/winn-dixie-plans-exit-326-locations-cutback
[3] https://www.richmondfed.org/publications/research/econ_focus/2005/summer/short_takes_web_exclusive2

More Competition, Less Families Spend on Food

The rise of supermarket grocers in the 20th century and the long list of competitive entrants that have since transformed the grocery industry have broadly resulted in a continuous reduction in the percentage of household income spent on food.

In 1901, Americans spent 43 percent of their income on food. Today, American households spend less of their income on food than ever before, with food costs constituting just 13 percent of household income, a reduction of over 70 percent since 1901.

FAMILIES IN THE UNITED STATES ARE CURRENTLY SPENDING LESS OF THEIR INCOME ON FOOD COMPARED TO ANY OTHER PERIOD IN THE LAST 100 YEARS

% OF FAMILY INCOME SPENT ON FOOD (U.S. 1901-2022)

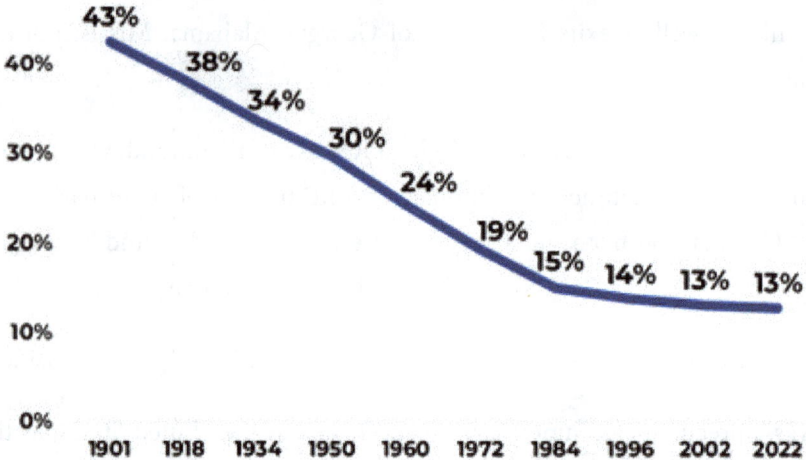

Year	Percentage
1901	43%
1918	38%
1934	34%
1950	30%
1960	24%
1972	19%
1984	15%
1996	14%
2002	13%
2022	13%

Source: BLS Consumer Expenditure Surveys

Falling Profits for Supermarket Grocers

At the start of the 21st century, as I was beginning my career, supermarket grocers' EBITDA margins were a staggering 40 percent higher than they are now. (EBITDA means earnings before interest, taxes, depreciation and amortization; it is a good proxy for cash flow.)

SUPERMARKET GROCER EBITDA MARGINS HAVE MEANINGFULLY DECLINED

HISTORIC SUPERMARKET GROCERS' EBITDA MARGIN

7.5%

40% higher in 2001 than 2023

5.4%

2001

2023[1]

Source: Capital IQ and Company filings as of September 2024. Includes A&P (until 2009), Albertsons, Ingles, Kroger, Roundy's (until 2015), Safeway (until 2014), Stater Bros (until 2013), Village and Weis.
1)LTM Figures.

In fact, most supermarket grocers' profit margins (profit being net income, after accounting for interest, taxes, depreciation and amortization) are only between 1.5 and 2.0 percent. Publix is an exception for reasons we will discuss later.

MOST SUPERMARKET GROCERS' PROFIT MARGINS ARE ONLY 1.5 – 2.0%

LTM PROFIT MARGIN (NET INCOME)

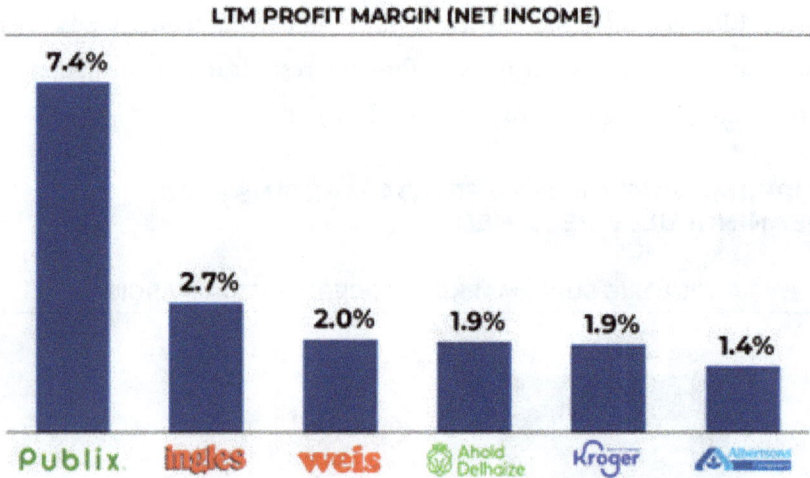

Source: Capital IQ and Company Filings as of September 2024

Food represents such a small portion of household income for the same reason supermarket grocery profit margins have declined so much: there is far more competition in American grocery than ever before, which has led to significant price reductions over time relative to cost inflation.

Grocery ≠ Supermarkets

Contrary to what remains a far-too-popular belief, **"grocery" does <u>not</u> equal "supermarkets."** Grocery equals super**<u>centers</u>**, plus club grocers, plus discount, dollar and drug grocers, plus specialty/ethnic and online grocers and, yes, supermarket grocers as well. <u>**They're all grocers**</u>. (This is why I refer to supermarkets as "supermarket grocers"; to emphasize the reality that supermarket grocers are just one of many different grocery formats where we shop.) I have spent several years trying to help numerous constituencies understand this basic fact.

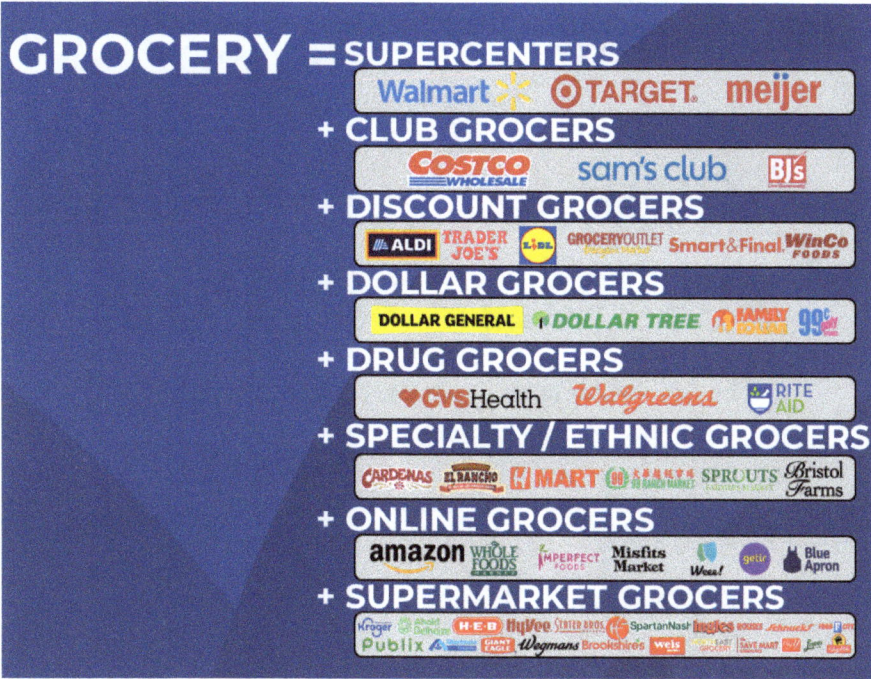

It remains shocking to me that while most people shop at so many different grocers on a regular basis, there seems to be cognitive dissonance (and willful blindness) about the grocery industry and supermarket grocers' shrinking portion of it.

The Rise of the National/Discount Grocers

For many years, I've been sounding the alarm about the rise of national/ discount grocers — Walmart/Sam's, Target/Shipt, Costco, Amazon/Whole Foods, Aldi, Trader Joe's, Dollar General and Family Dollar/Dollar Tree, among others — and the existential threat they pose to supermarket grocers. This risk is not theoretical; we have all witnessed very similar dynamics with America's department stores, which have been marginalized over the past 20-plus years in the general merchandise industry by some of the same forces, which include the world's largest grocers (which are also some of the world's largest retailers).

NATIONAL / DISCOUNT GROCERS HAVE TRANSFORMED AMERICAN GROCERY

NATIONAL / DISCOUNT GROCERS

Transformation of the Top 15 U.S. Grocers

Twenty years ago, 10 of the top 15 American grocers were supermarket grocers. Walmart was America's #1 grocer by sales, but Kroger — America's largest supermarket grocer — was only $24 billion behind. (I know $24 billion seems like a big number, but I'd ask you to hold that thought for a moment.) Costco and Target were not too focused on grocery yet, so they weren't terribly high in the rankings. Both A&P — the Walmart of American grocery in the 1950s and 1960s, with over 15,000 stores — and Winn-Dixie were still top grocers; they have both since gone bankrupt and have been acquired in pieces.

Look who's not on the list: Amazon was focused primarily on books and barely sold groceries; it was 14 years away from buying Whole Foods. Dollar General, Family Dollar, Aldi and Trader Joe's were much smaller. Online grocery was still developing.

20 YEARS AGO, SUPERMARKET GROCERS COMPRISED 10 OF THE TOP 15 U.S. GROCERS

($ In Billions)

U.S. GROCERS – 2003   **NOT ON THE LIST**

Ranking	Company	Grocery Sales	% Market Share
1	Walmart / sam's club	$73	16%
2	Kroger	$49	11%
3	Albertsons	$32	7%
4	SAFEWAY	$28	6%
5	Ahold USA	$24	5%
6	COSTCO WHOLESALE	$20	4%
7	DELHAIZE AMERICA	$14	3%
8	Publix	$14	3%
9	TARGET	$11	2%
10	Winn Dixie	$10	2%
11	SUPERVALU	$10	2%
12	A&P	$10	2%
13	H-E-B	$8	2%
14	CVS Health	$8	2%
15	meijer	$7	1%

National / Discount Grocers

NOT ON THE LIST: amazon, WHOLE FOODS, DOLLAR GENERAL, DOLLAR TREE, FAMILY DOLLAR, ALDI, TRADER JOE'S, Walgreens, SPROUTS FARMERS MARKET, THE FRESH MARKET, GOOD FOOD HOLDINGS, FRESH THYME MARKET, HERITAGE GROCERS GROUP, CARDENAS, TONY'S, EL RANCHO, H MART, 99 RANCH MARKET

Source: Company filings and publicly available information.
Note: Represents U.S. grocery sales only and excludes pharmacy, fuel and other non-grocery categories.

Today, the entire industry has flipped: only five of the top 15 grocers are supermarket grocers; ten are national/discount grocers. Walmart now has **over $200 billion more** in U.S. grocery sales than Kroger, not just $24 billion more. Costco and Target have catapulted up the rankings. Amazon has now surpassed Albertsons as the #4 U.S. grocer and is growing very rapidly. Dollar General, Aldi, Family Dollar/Dollar Tree, Walgreens and Trader Joc's all have prominent positions as they continue to accelerate their grocery businesses.

TODAY, SUPERMARKETS ARE ONLY 5 OF THE TOP 15 U.S. GROCERS; 10 ARE NATIONAL / DISCOUNT GROCERS

($ In Billions)

U.S. GROCERS – 2023

Ranking	Company	Grocery Sales	% Market Share
1	Walmart	$328 ⎤ $215bn	30%
2	Kroger	$113 ⎦	10%
3	COSTCO WHOLESALE	$100	9%
4	amazon WHOLE FOODS	$67	6%
5	Albertsons	$65	6%
6	TARGET. Shipt	$56	5%
7	Ahold Delhaize	$51	5%
8	Publix	$48	4%
9	H-E-B	$34	3%
10	DOLLAR GENERAL	$32	3%
11	ALDI	$29	3%
12	CVS Health	$22	2%
13	DOLLAR TREE FAMILY DOLLAR	$19	2%
14	Walgreens	$16	1%
15	TRADER JOE'S	$16	1%

National / Discount Grocers

Source: Company filings as of September 2024 and the Mercatus Grocery Insights Report.
Note: U.S. grocery sales excludes pharmacy, fuel and other non-grocery categories. Amazon figures reflect 90% of North America sales (U.S. not reported). Aldi figures include the recent acquisition of Winn Dixie and Harveys stores.

According to FMI, the leading U.S. grocery trade organization, supermarket grocers 20 years ago were the "primary shop" for 79 percent of Americans. In 2023, it was down to 38 percent, a 41 percent decrease. Meanwhile, national/discount grocers have nearly tripled over the last 20 years, from 21 percent to 62 percent.[4]

---

[4] Source: FMI U.S. Grocery Shopper Trends: 2003 and 2023.

AS SHOPPERS' PRIMARY GROCERY CHANNEL NATIONAL / DISCOUNT GROCERS HAVE NEARLY TRIPLED IN 20 YEARS

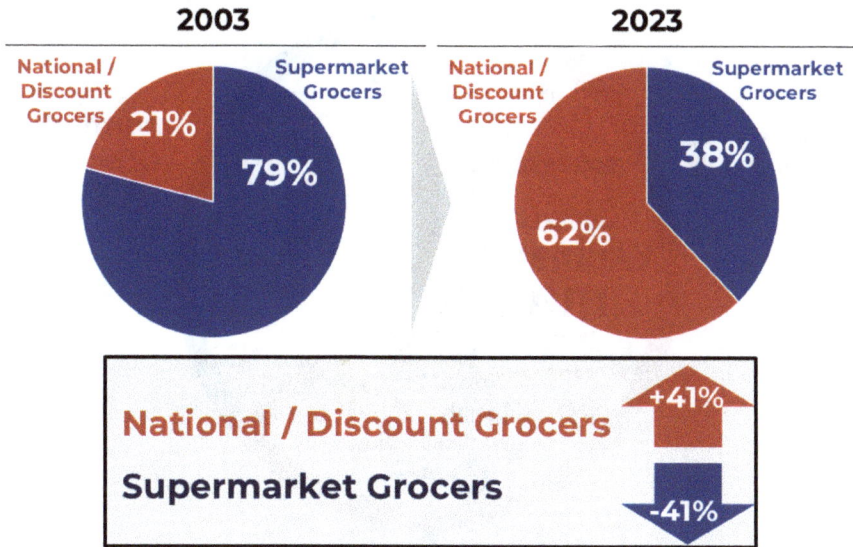

2003

National / Discount Grocers **21%**

Supermarket Grocers **79%**

2023

National / Discount Grocers **62%**

Supermarket Grocers **38%**

National / Discount Grocers **+41%**

Supermarket Grocers **-41%**

Source: FMI U.S. Grocery Shopper Trends: 2003 and 2023.

National/Discount Grocers Dominate U.S. Grocery Market Share

As a result of all these changes, national/discount grocers, all of which are mostly, if not entirely, non-union, have over 60 percent grocery share. There are still no national supermarket grocers even with the pending Kroger/Albertsons merger.

TODAY, ENORMOUS NATIONAL / DISCOUNT GROCERS CONTROL WELL OVER 60% OF THE U.S. GROCERY MARKET

National / Discount Grocers 66%

Supermarket Grocers 34%

Source: Company filings as of September 2024 and the Mercatus Grocery Insights Report.
Note: U.S. grocery sales excludes pharmacy, fuel and other non-grocery categories. Amazon figures reflect 90% of North America sales (U.S. not reported). Pro forma for Winn Dixie and Harveys stores recently acquired.

Over the past 20 years, there have been stark changes in grocery market share. Walmart's share is up 13 percent; Amazon and Costco are up five percent; Target is up three percent; Dollar General and Aldi are each up two percent. Conversely, Kroger is down one percent; Ahold Delhaize is down two percent (mind you, this is after combining in 2016); Albertsons is down seven percent (notwithstanding its acquisition of Safeway in 2015). **The national/discount grocers have gained over 30 percent share in total**.

WALMART, AMAZON, COSTCO, TARGET, DG AND ALDI (ALL NON-UNION) HAVE TAKEN LOTS OF GROCERY SHARE

GROCERY SHARE CHANGE (2003-2023)

This phenomenon is not isolated to certain markets, but rather is clearly pervasive across the country. In reviewing the top 25 U.S. markets by population, there is a similarly stark difference between the share gains that Walmart and Costco have generated in markets across the country versus the share losses that Kroger and Albertsons have experienced.

NATIONAL / DISCOUNT GROCERS SHARE IN THE MOST POPULOUS MARKETS IS SURGING AS WELL (2012-2022)

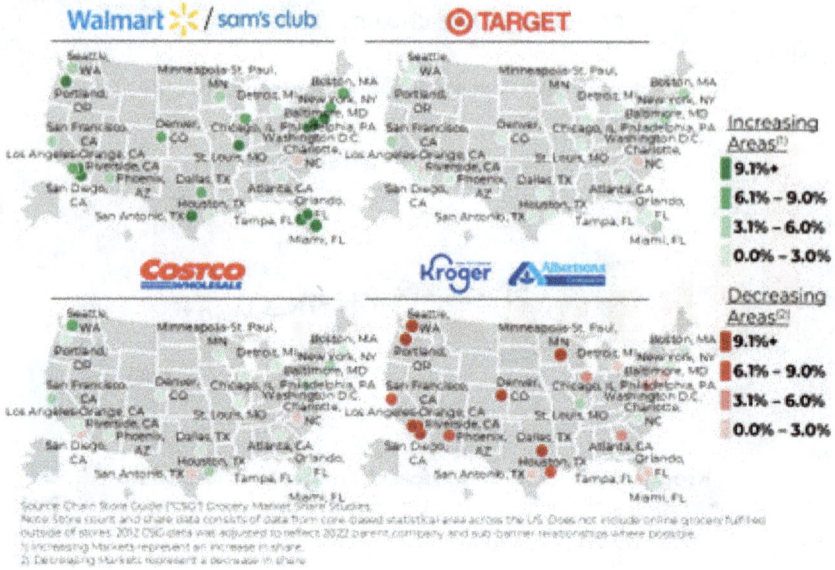

Source: Chain Store Guide (CSG) Grocery Market Share Studies.
Note: Store counts and share data consists of data from core based statistical area across the US. Does not include online grocery fulfilled outside of stores. 2012 CSG data was adjusted to reflect 2022 parent company and sub-banner relationships where possible.
1) Increasing Markets represent an increase in share.
2) Decreasing Markets represent a decrease in share.

The transformation of American grocery in the past 20 years has been driven by three clear factors: 1) an exponential increase in the number of national/discount grocers, 2) consumers' abandonment of one-stop grocery shopping and 3) the rise of online grocery. There is more consumer choice, convenience, competition and price transparency than ever before.

National/Discount Grocers Have Many More Stores Than Supermarket Grocers

There are now over 70,000 national/discount grocers in the United States, many of which were not grocery competitors a generation ago, including: ~7,000 supercenters (Walmart, Target and Meijer); ~1,400 clubs (Costco, Sam's and BJs); ~37,000 dollar grocers (that's just Dollar General and Dollar Tree/Family Dollar), ~20,000 drug stores (that's just Walgreens, CVS and Rite Aid); ~4,000 discount grocers (Germany's Aldi and Trader Joe's, Grocery Outlet, Save A Lot and, more recently, Germany's Lidl).

NATIONAL / DISCOUNT GROCERS' GROWTH FAR EXCEEDS THAT OF SUPERMARKET GROCERS

U.S. STORE BASE GROWTH BY RETAIL CONCEPT (2013 – 2023)

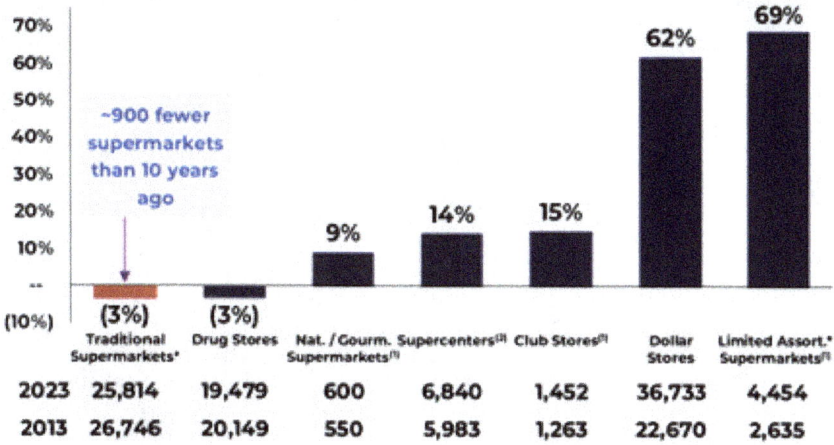

	Traditional Supermarkets*	Drug Stores	Nat. / Gourm. Supermarkets[1]	Supercenters[2]	Club Stores[1]	Dollar Stores	Limited Assort.* Supermarkets[1]
2023	25,814	19,479	600	6,840	1,452	36,733	4,454
2013	26,746	20,149	550	5,983	1,263	22,670	2,635

Source: Progressive Grocer Annual Report of the Grocery Industry, Public Filings and SP estimates
Note: * indicates > $2M in annual sales.
1) Includes public companies only.
2) Includes Meijer, Target and Walmart

Over the past 20 years, the number of national/discount grocery stores has more than doubled, growing by over 38,000 stores from roughly 32,000 to over 70,000 (a 121 percent increase). Discount grocers, including the dollar grocers, Grocery Outlet and the German hard discounters Aldi and Lidl, have roughly *tripled* their store bases from under 14,000 to over 40,000 stores.

NATIONAL / DISCOUNT GROCERS' HAVE MORE THAN DOUBLED THEIR STORE BASE AND TRANSFORMED U.S. GROCERY

NATIONAL / DISCOUNT GROCERS' STORE COUNT GROWTH

Source: Company Filings, Company Websites & Equity Research as of September 2024.

As a result of these challenges, there are now less than 26,000 traditional supermarkets in the United States, roughly 900 fewer than 10 years ago and 2,300 fewer than 20 years ago. Regional supermarkets have been slowly eclipsed by the shadow of various extremely large, well-capitalized (investment grade), non-union and fast-growing national/discount grocers.

THE NUMBER OF SUPERMARKETS HAS DECLINED BY MORE THAN 8% IN THE PAST 20 YEARS

NUMBER OF SUPERMARKETS (2003-2023)

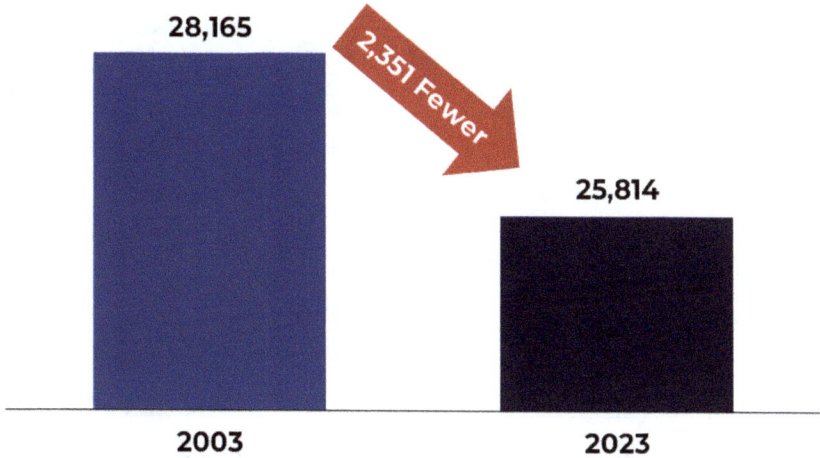

28,165

2,351 Fewer

25,814

2003   2023

Source: Progressive Grocer Annual Report of the Grocery Industry, FMI, Public filings and Solomon Partners estimates.
Note: Supermarkets includes conventional supermarkets.

The End of One-Stop Grocery Shopping

The second key change is the end of one-stop grocery shopping. With the exponential rise in grocery choice with over 38,000 more national/discount grocery store entrants, and customer acquisition being funded by these large global grocers, the average consumer now shops for groceries every week at more than five different grocers, in four different grocery channels (e.g., supermarkets, supercenters, drug stores, discount/dollar grocers, club stores and various specialty grocers), a 44 percent increase over 2014, according to FMI.

NATIONAL / DISCOUNT GROCERS' EXTREME STORE GROWTH AND BROAD CUSTOMER TRIP DISPERSION HAVE TRANSFORMED U.S. GROCERY

CONSUMERS REGULARLY SHOP 4 GROCERY TYPES & 5 BANNERS

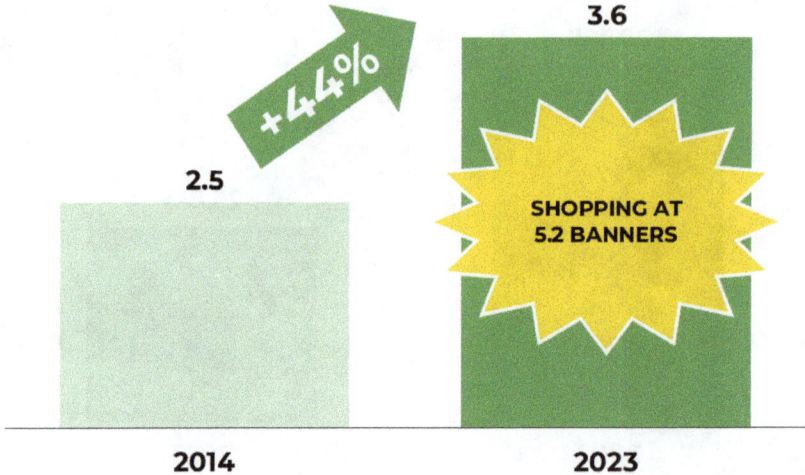

+44%

3.6

2.5

SHOPPING AT 5.2 BANNERS

2014

2023

Source: FMI U.S. Grocery Shopper Trends 2014 and 2023.

"Consumers have more options than ever before when it comes to their grocery shopping," confirms Amanda Schoenbauer, an analyst at data company Numerator. They *"can more easily switch up where they shop to take advantage of deals and to capitalize on convenience."*[5]

According to Numerator, the average shopper purchased groceries at 20.7 unique retailers between March 2023 and February 2024. *"I haven't [one-stop] shopped in years,"* one grocery customer recently told Axios.[6]

---

[5] https://www.axios.com/2024/06/10/grocery-store-shopping-costco-aldi-kroger-walmart
[6] Ibid.

Online Grocery's Great Leap Forward

The third key factor transforming American grocery is that online grocery has quadrupled in the past four years since Covid initially hit, led not by supermarket grocers, but by Walmart, Target, Costco and Amazon.

ONLINE GROCERY HAS QUADRUPLED SINCE COVID

ONLINE GROCERY HAS INCREASED 4X

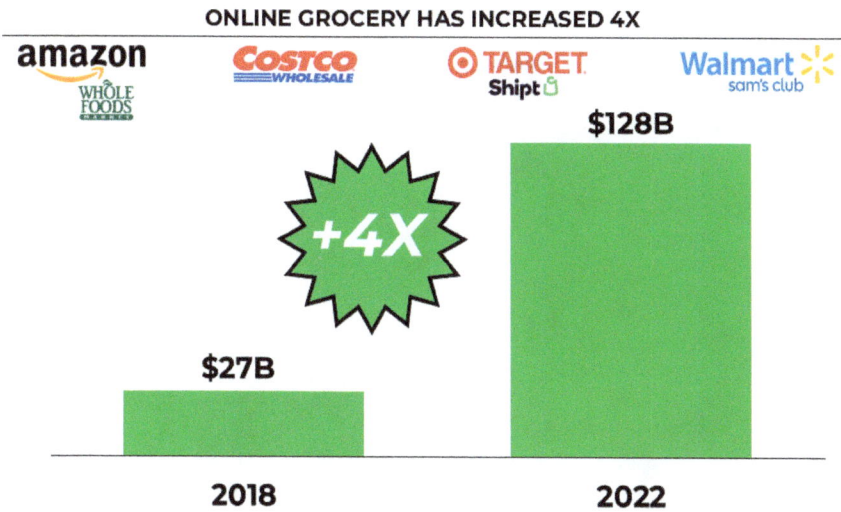

$128B

+4X

$27B

2018   2022

Source: FMI U.S. Grocery Shopper Trends: 2003, 2014, 2023, Progressive Grocer, Mercatus and Incisive Grocery.

＊ ＊ ＊

In the past few years, millions of store teammates were heroes as they helped to safely feed America during the pandemic. But during that time, notwithstanding short-term increases in demand while restaurants were temporarily shut down, the extent to which their stores were falling behind their larger peers, the national/discount grocers, was palpable.

Throughout the pandemic, the national/discount grocers leveraged their massive scale in order to secure supply allocation advantages to better stock their shelves and renovate their stores; they increased marketing and technology investments to drive customer acquisition and retention; and they offered higher wages and better benefits to fulfill their employment needs, all of which was challenging for smaller, regional supermarket grocers to profitably match.

In the next chapter, we will look in more detail at the forces of dislocation that are shaping Supermarkets Present.

CHAPTER 2

The Ghost of Supermarkets Present

In May 2024, Jim Cramer made an astounding declaration on CNBC's *Squawk on the Street*: **"There is a 'big three' for food, and food drives people…Costco, Amazon, Walmart…the 'big three' of food."**

No supermarket grocers — just three global behemoths that sell more groceries than almost anyone.

This was consistent with what I had been saying in countless presentations over the better part of two decades, effectively shouting from America's grocery rooftops about the ways our industry was changing.

"There is a 'big three' for food, and food drives people… **Costco, Amazon, Walmart** *… the* **'big three' of food***."*

- *Jim Cramer, CNBC's Squawk on the Street*

Today, the national/discount grocers have roughly $700 billion in total U.S. grocery sales, while supermarket grocers only have about $400 billion. Interestingly, Walmart's $320+ billion U.S. grocery business is almost as large as all supermarket grocers combined. More on them shortly.

NATIONAL / DISCOUNT GROCERS ACCOUNT FOR FAR MORE GROCERY SALES THAN SUPERMARKET GROCERS

($ in Billions) **U.S. GROCERY SALES**

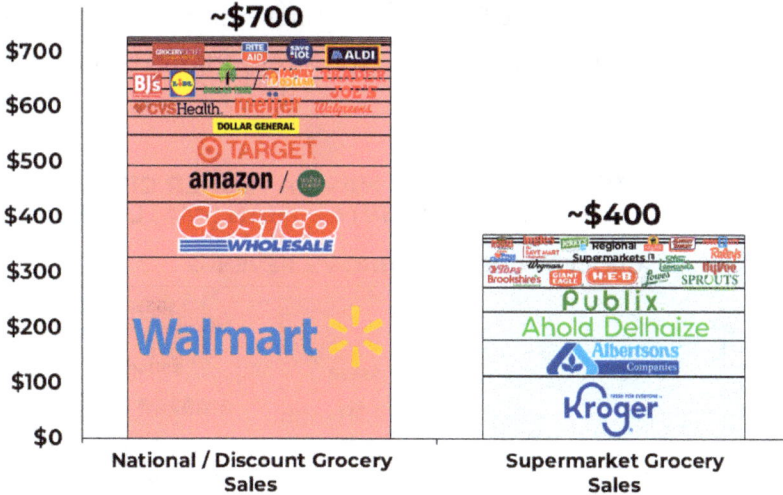

Source: Company filings and publicly available information as of September 2024.
1) Regional Supermarkets includes rest of the Top 100 grocers not already covered on the list and assumes 90% Food & Consumables.

How did we get here? How are so many supermarket grocers being squeezed out of Supermarkets Present?

It starts with something you don't read about too often in the press but is actually the foundation of the current state of American grocery: relative cost of capital.

National/Discount Grocers' Low Cost of Capital

There is a strong correlation between scale and credit rating. Statistically, roughly 60 percent of credit rating is driven by company sales. Look at our sector's public operators: there is a clear relationship between scale and credit rating. Here's how it works: bigger sales mean a better rating, which means cheaper debt, which facilitates more investment in price, wages, marketing, technology and growth. That's how you acquire and retain customers, which is ultimately how to succeed in retail.

As we will review shortly, Walmart generates over $660 billion in annual sales globally and has an AA credit rating; this enables the company to borrow cheaper than most countries. Large banks will all but beg to underwrite their debt issuances, in many cases effectively losing money to do so. Supermarket grocers' debt is generally much more expensive, particularly for smaller regional operators.

LARGER OPERATORS GENERALLY HAVE A HIGHER CREDIT RATING AND LOWER COST OF CAPITAL THAN SMALLER PEERS

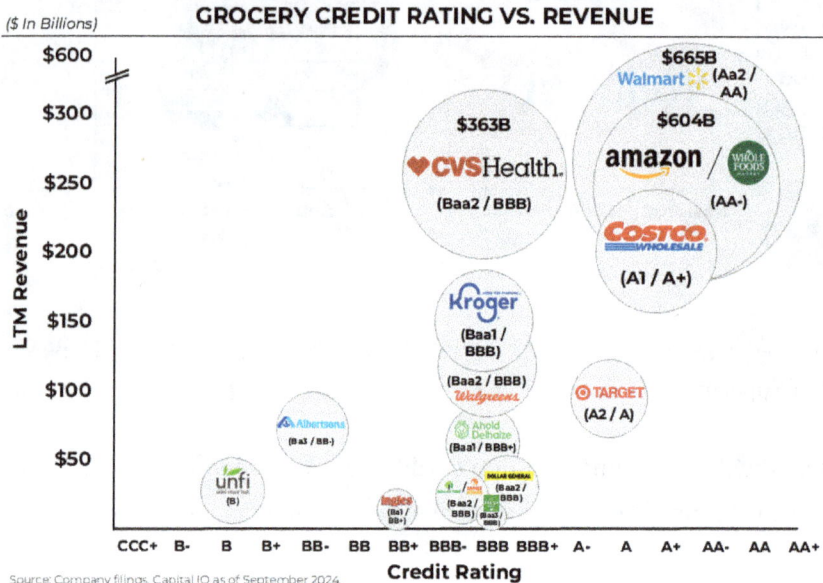

GROCERY CREDIT RATING VS. REVENUE

($ In Billions)

Walmart $665B (Aa2 / AA)

$363B CVSHealth. (Baa2 / BBB)

$604B amazon / WHOLE FOODS (AA-)

COSTCO WHOLESALE (A1 / A+)

Kroger (Baa1 / BBB)

(Baa2 / BBB) Walgreens

TARGET (A2 / A)

Albertsons (Ba3 / BB-)

Ahold Delhaize (Baa1 / BBB+)

unfi (B)

Ingles (Ba1 / BB+)

(Baa2 / BBB) (Ba3 / BB+)

DOLLAR GENERAL (Baa2 / BBB)

LTM Revenue: $600, $300, $250, $200, $150, $100, $50

Credit Rating: CCC+ B- B B+ BB- BB BB+ BBB- BBB BBB+ A- A A+ AA- AA AA+

Source: Company filings, Capital IQ as of September 2024.

A lower cost of capital is how Walmart and other national/discount grocers like Target, Costco, Aldi and Dollar General drive their grocery market share with lower prices, higher wages, more marketing spending, increased technology investments and more growth.

All of these operational investments are facilitated by scale efficiencies, including lower cost of goods. This has, in turn, forced traditional supermarket grocers to lower their prices in order to retain some share of the average household's various weekly grocery trips. This, again, is a key reason why the proportion of food cost to household income has declined so much over time.

While the largest supermarket grocers can endure some price investment, the vast majority of smaller regional supermarkets lost a significant percentage of their annual cash flow in the few years before Covid trying to keep up (many lost 20 percent-40 percent of their EBITDA). This decline meaningfully impacted the ability of these grocers to match their national peers' operational investments and continue to remain profitable, particularly as labor and technology cost inflation has skyrocketed. This led to numerous supermarket grocery bankruptcies, which we will review later.

Walmart

Walmart is the world's largest grocer by a staggering extent, with over $400 billion in global grocery sales, three times more than anyone else operating in the United States.

WALMART IS THE WORLD'S #1 GROCER AND HAS 3X MORE GLOBAL GROCERY SALES THAN ANY OTHER U.S. OPERATOR

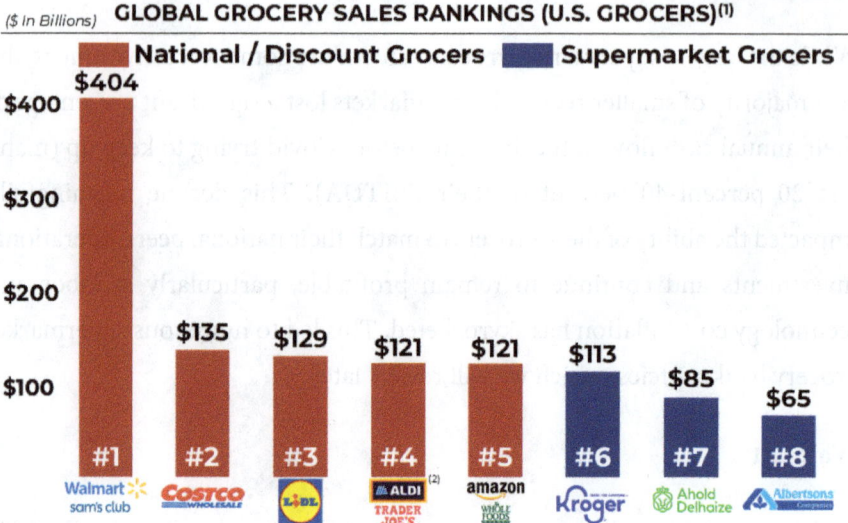

($ in Billions) **GLOBAL GROCERY SALES RANKINGS (U.S. GROCERS)[1]**

National / Discount Grocers   Supermarket Grocers

$404	$135	$129	$121	$121	$113	$85	$65
#1	#2	#3	#4 [2]	#5	#6	#7	#8
Walmart sam's club	COSTCO WHOLESALE	LIDL	ALDI TRADER JOE'S	amazon WHOLE FOODS	Kroger	Ahold Delhaize	Albertsons Companies

Source: Company Filings & Company Websites as of September 2024.
1)Among grocers with operations in the U.S.
2)Includes Aldi Sud 2023 & Aldi Nord 2022 figures, which represents the latest publicly available information. Pro forma for Winn Dixie and Harveys stores recently acquired.

In addition to a very low cost of capital, Walmart's business model itself creates a significant competitive advantage vis-à-vis supermarket grocers. Walmart uses higher-margin general merchandise such as clothes, housewares, toys and sporting goods to subsidize lower prices on groceries, which attracts customers to shop there more regularly. Since they are already in the store to buy groceries, more customers buy Walmart's general merchandise more often; these general merchandise sales — and their strong gross profit — drive this powerful flywheel.

Another important driver for Walmart is its broad productivity loop. Having over $660 billion in total global sales — well over a half *trillion* dollars — enables the company to spread its fixed costs over a much larger sales base. This generates more excess cash flow, which can then be used to make more investments in price, which solidifies the loyalty of its customers, who then buy even more — strengthening the productivity loop.

Walmart has built a ubiquitous store base, with over 10,600 stores globally and over 5,200 in the U.S., including roughly 600 Sam's Clubs. (Some people suggest Walmart and Sam's grocery sales should not be aggregated because they are two different companies, notwithstanding the same ownership. Given they have merged their supply chain teams to derive clear benefits from their scale, it seems appropriate to combine them.[7])

The company likes to boast that over 90 percent of Americans live within 10 miles of a Walmart. Most of their sales — over 60 percent — are groceries.

Walmart now has a $328 billion U.S. grocery business, which has quadrupled in the past 20 years. The company now has roughly 30 percent national grocery market share, ***nearly as much as the 34 percent that all supermarket grocers have, combined***.

WALMART HAS NEARLY AS MUCH U.S. GROCERY SHARE AS ALL SUPERMARKET GROCERS _COMBINED_

U.S. GROCERY MARKET SHARE

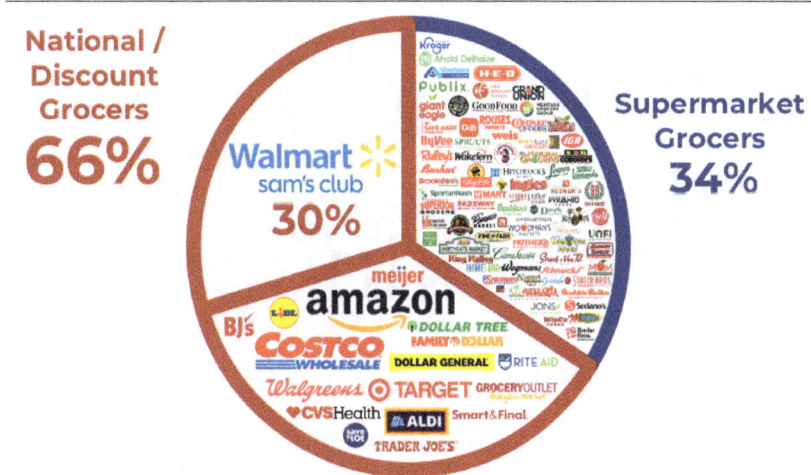

Source: Company filings and Capital IQ as of September 2024.
Note: Reflects annual U.S. grocery sales, excluding pharmacy, fuel and other non-grocery categories. Amazon figures reflect 90% of North America sales (U.S. not reported). Aldi figures include the recent acquisition of Winn Dixie and Harveys stores.

---

[7] https://www.supermarketnews.com/retail-labor/sam-s-club-and-walmart-supply-chain-teams-to-merge

Walmart's grocery business is three times the size of Kroger (which operates only in the United States); three times Costco's U.S grocery business; five times Albertsons (which also only operates in the U.S.); and five times Amazon.

To provide a sense of scale, that's over 20 times the sales of Trader Joe's and over 90 times the sales of Ingles, a family-owned grocer in the Carolinas with roughly $4 billion in grocery sales (almost $6 billion in total sales) that would be considered a pretty large company on almost any scale, but not in U.S. grocery.

WALMART, AMERICA'S #1 GROCER, HAS U.S. GROCERY SALES THAT ARE MANY TIMES ITS GROCERY COMPETITORS

U.S. GROCERY SALES

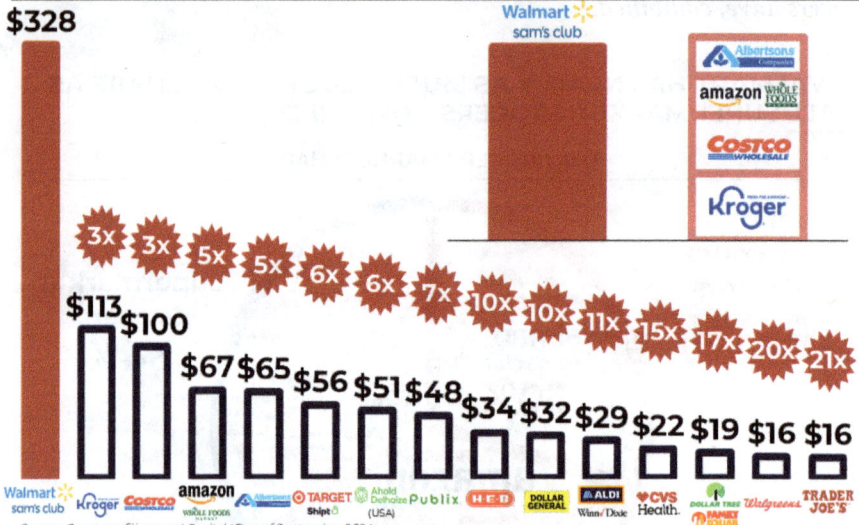

($ In Billions)

$328

Walmart sam's club

3x $113
3x $100
5x $67
5x $65
6x $56
6x $51
7x $48
10x $34
10x $32
11x $29
15x $22
17x $19
20x $16
21x $16

Walmart sam's club | Kroger | Costco | amazon WHOLE FOODS MARKET | Albertsons | TARGET Shipt (USA) | Ahold Delhaize | Publix | H-E-B | DOLLAR GENERAL Winn/Dixie | ALDI | CVS Health. | DOLLAR TREE FAMILY DOLLAR | Walgreens | TRADER JOE'S

Source: Company filings and Capital IQ as of September 2024.
Note: Reflects annual U.S. grocery sales, excluding pharmacy, fuel and other non-grocery categories. Amazon figures reflect 90% of North America sales (U.S. not reported). Aldi figures include the recent acquisition of Winn Dixie and Harveys stores.

Perhaps most staggering is that Walmart's U.S. grocery business is roughly as large as that of all of its next four competitors — Kroger, Costco, Albertsons and Amazon — *combined*.

WALMART'S U.S. GROCERY SALES ARE ROUGHLY THE SAME AS KROGER, COSTCO, AMAZON AND ALBERTSONS, THE NEXT FOUR U.S. GROCERS <u>COMBINED</u>

U.S. GROCERY SALES

Source: Company filings and Capital IQ as of September 2024.
Note: Reflects annual U.S. grocery sales, excluding pharmacy, fuel and other non-grocery categories. Amazon figures reflect 90% of North America sales (U.S. not reported).

When you look more granularly at Walmart's market share across the country, the numbers somehow get even more extreme. Walmart has over 50 percent market share in nearly 300 U.S. markets, roughly one-third of the markets where it operates; it has over 40 percent market share in nearly 500 U.S. markets, 55 percent of the markets where it operates; it has over 30 percent market share in 700 U.S. markets, nearly 80 percent of the markets in which it operates. These are just staggering figures.

WALMART, AMERICA'S #1 GROCER, IS UBIQUITOUS, Walmart
WITH OVER 40% SHARE IN NEARLY 500 MARKETS

WALMART U.S. GROCERY MARKET SHARE

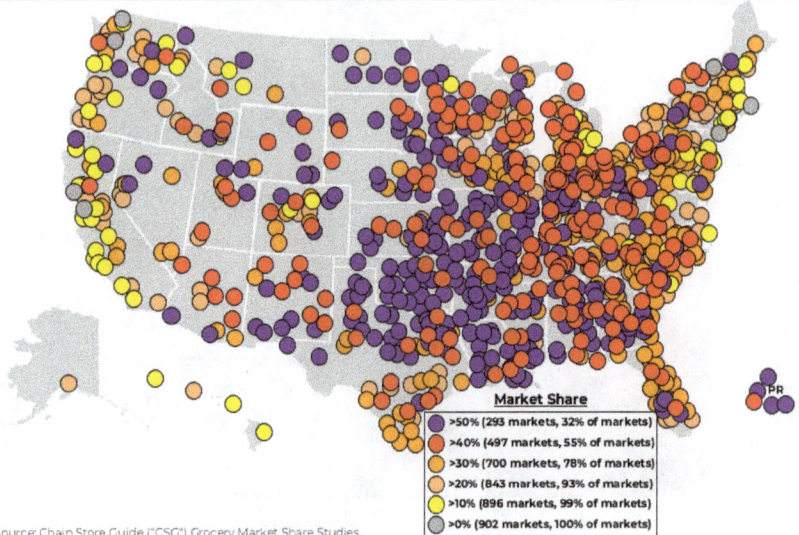

Market Share
- >50% (293 markets, 32% of markets)
- >40% (497 markets, 55% of markets)
- >30% (700 markets, 78% of markets)
- >20% (843 markets, 93% of markets)
- >10% (896 markets, 99% of markets)
- >0% (902 markets, 100% of markets)

Source: Chain Store Guide ("CSG") Grocery Market Share Studies.
Note: Market share data consists of data from core-based statistical area across the US. Does not include online grocery fulfilled outside of stores.

But they're not done. Walmart's CEO Doug McMillon said in the company's first-quarter fiscal year 2024 earnings call:

We continue to gain market share in the grocery category, including with higher income and younger shoppers, and we saw good growth in membership income in both businesses. At Sam's Club U.S., member count and Plus member penetration hit all-time highs in the quarter. Our growth is now being driven by convenience in addition to price. We see it across formats and in common age cohorts.[8]

---

[8] https://www.fool.com/earnings/call-transcripts/2023/05/18/walmart-wmt-q1-2024-earnings-call-transcript/

As various grocers try to use private label to differentiate and offer a lower price alternative to national brands, Walmart carries the top five private-label brands in the United States.[9]

And Walmart continues to grow. They plan to open or expand 150 stores in the next five years, on top of 650 remodels in 2024, which is on top of the $9 billion they've already spent on 1,400 store upgrades in the last two years. It is simply not possible for supermarket grocers to keep up.

THE WALL STREET JOURNAL.

Walmart, in a Reversal, to Open New Stores in the U.S.
January 31, 2024 9:00 AM

"The retail giant plans to open or expand 150 stores in the U.S. over the next five years...

...Walmart...also plans to remodel around 650 of its U.S. locations over the next 12 months...

...That is on top of upgrades to around 1,400 stores over the last two years, an effort that the company said cost around $9 billion."

Walmart has broadened the portion of the socio-economic spectrum where it focuses well beyond its traditional lower-income customer base. This has been meaningfully enhanced by its development of Walmart+, Walmart's response to Amazon Prime (which we will discuss later). A recent Morgan Stanley

---

[9] https://www.supermarketnews.com/private-label/walmart-owns-top-5-private-label-brands

survey suggests that Walmart+ now has 17 percent household penetration.[10] According to Prosper Insights & Analytics, 28 percent of U.S. households with at least $150,000 in annual income were members of Walmart+ in 2023, up from 13 percent in 2022 (to be fair, Amazon Prime still has a commanding lead with 77 percent of those households).[11]

Walmart's customer acquisition efforts have also been buffeted by its acquisition of Jet.com, whose founder, Mark Lore, stayed on long enough to transform Walmart's e-commerce and online grocery business (which we will also discuss later).

Walmart has also built a large retail advertising platform to help offset costs even more. According to MediaPost, Walmart's advertising business is a $3.4 billion juggernaut, growing at 20 to 25 percent annually, with very high margins.[12] Walmart has replicated Amazon's marketplace to add more third-party sellers and drive e-commerce and advertising revenue, including outside the U.S. in places like India, where Walmart has spent billions of dollars on its meaningful stake in Flipkart.

Walmart's $2.3 billion acquisition of VIZIO in 2024 will further support the broad consumer and third-party seller ecosystem Walmart is building. As Walmart noted on its website:

> *The acquisition of VIZIO and its SmartCast Operating System (OS) would enable Walmart to connect with and serve its customers in new ways including innovative television and in-home entertainment and media experiences. It would also create new opportunities to help*

---

[10] https://www.investing.com/news/stock-market-news/morgan-stanley-survey-points-to-record-215m-walmart-members-432SI-3113514

[11] https://www.digitalcommerce360.com/2023/03/09/walmart-chips-away-at-amazons-lead-in-a-key-area-wealthy-online-shoppers

[12] https://www.mediapost.com/publications/article/397361/report-walmarts-growing-ad-strength-shakes-up-it.html

advertisers connect with customers, empowering brands with differentiated and compelling opportunities to engage at scale and to realize greater impact from their advertising spend with Walmart. The combination would be expected to further accelerate Walmart's media business in the U.S., Walmart Connect, bringing together VIZIO's advertising solutions business with Walmart's reach and capabilities. These benefits would be further strengthened by the growth of connected TV platforms and Walmart's industry-leading TV panel sales.[13]

In short, Walmart dominates American grocery to an extent many (likely most) people just don't appreciate.

Costco

Costco is an extraordinary company in an exceptional retail and grocery channel. Like Walmart, clubs use extensive general merchandise offerings to subsidize their grocery business, which accounts for most of Costco's sales and drives regular customer traffic. The major difference with Walmart is that the foundation of Costco's business model is its recurring membership fee base, which generates $5 billion in annual revenue, nearly half of its cash flow.

Warehouse clubs like Costco display products in full-pallet format (as they look when unloaded from trucks), which limits the need for individual units to be placed on shelves. This results in higher sales per labor hour and less labor generally than supermarket grocers. Clubs are also mostly non-union, which means lower-cost labor than most supermarkets. Because most goods are offered in bulk, clubs are considered to be low-cost alternatives to traditional supermarket grocers. With Costco beating Trader Joe's as America's favorite

---

[13] https://corporate.walmart.com/news/2024/02/20/walmart-agrees-to-acquire-vizio-holding-corp-to-facilitate-accelerated-growth-of-walmart-connect-through-vizio-s-smartcast-operating-system

grocer in a recent customer satisfaction study, it is very clear that customers love shopping for groceries there.

CNBC

Costco Has Replaced Trader Joe's as America's Favorite Supermarket

February 9, 2024 12:09 PM

"...[Costco] tied for first with Publix and H-E-B in the annual American Customer Satisfaction Index Retail and Consumer Shipping Study..."

Club stores are growing rapidly. The U.S. warehouse club channel has grown at 7 percent CAGR (compounded annual growth rate) since 2013, more than twice that of supermarket grocers. BJ's plans to open 10 new clubs per year, versus 10 cumulative openings from 2016 to 2020. Sam's Club announced plans to open 30 new clubs in next few years. Club stores are also poised for significant e-commerce growth.

CLUB STORES HAVE GROWN AT A RATE MORE THAN 2X THAT OF SUPERMARKET GROCERS OVER THE PAST 10 YEARS

10-YEAR SALES CAGR (CLUB STORES VS. SUPERMARKET GROCERS)

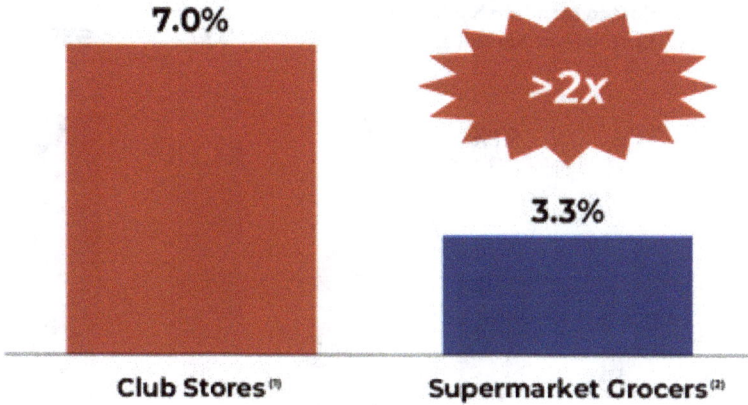

7.0%

>2x

3.3%

Club Stores [1]　　　　　　　**Supermarket Grocers** [2]

Source: Company filings as of September 2024
1) Includes Costco, Sam's Club and BJ's
2) Includes Kroger, Publix, Safeway (until 2014), Albertsons, Ahold USA, Delhaize (until 2017), Great A&P (until 2010), Stater Bros (until 2013), Harris Teeter (until 2012), Roundy's (until 2015), Ingles, Weis, Village, Arden (until 2012) and Tops (until 2016).

Since membership subscription is such an important component of the club store business model, renewal rates are very important. Costco, BJs and Walmart's Sam's Club have experienced record membership renewal rates in the past few years, resulting from the shift in consumer spending amid elevated inflation.

Each of Costco and BJ's has recently had at least 90 percent membership renewal rates, the continuous growth of which demonstrates the momentum in customer loyalty to the club grocer model.

COSTCO'S EXTRAORDINARY MEMBERSHIP REVENUE IS ~~Costco~~
DRIVEN BY AN EXCEPTIONAL (GROWING) RENEWAL RATE

COSTCO HAS HAD INCREASING MEMBERSHIP RETENTION AND REVENUE

COSTCO MEMBERSHIP REVENUE AND MEMBERSHIP RENEWAL RATES

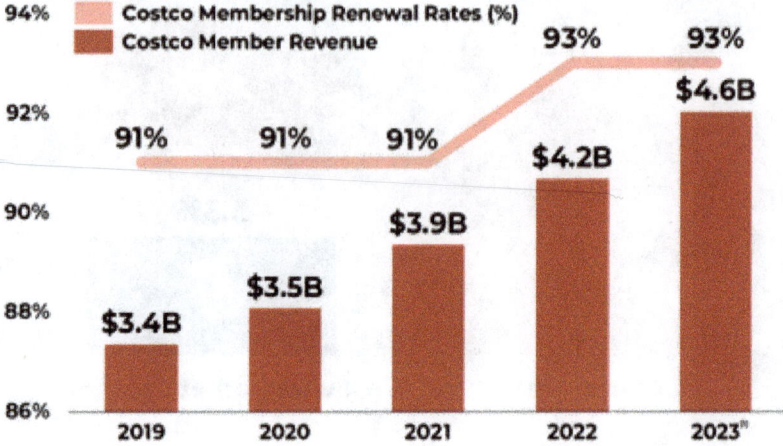

Source: Publicly available information and Capital IQ.
1) Reflects most recent available LTM data.

Since people want to get their money's worth on their membership, clubs have been siphoning grocery market share from traditional supermarkets, according to a report by CFRA Research. Club stores have outperformed traditional supermarkets in sales growth, with 10-year average comparable store sales growth over 200 basis points (2 percent) higher than supermarket grocers, particularly in recent years.

**CLUB STORE COMPS EXCEED SUPERMARKET GROCER
COMPS AND REMAIN HIGHLY ELEVATED**

COMPARABLE STORE SALES GROWTH (%) (2014 – PRESENT)

Costco is the #2-ranked grocer in the world, generating $135 billion in global grocery sales. It has 134 million members across the world, with 882 stores in the United States, Canada, United Kingdom, Taiwan, South Korea, Japan, Australia, Mexico, Spain, China, France, Iceland, New Zealand and Sweden. This is up from 433 roughly 20 years ago, when Costco was mostly in North America and the U.K. (with a few stores in Taiwan, Korea and Japan). This global scale has helped Costco continue to elevate its merchandise offering, particularly in grocery.

COSTCO IS THE WORLD'S #2 GROCER AND #3 U.S. GROCER

COSTCO'S U.S. GROCERY BUSINESS GENERATES ~$100 BILLION IN GROCERY SALES; ~40% OF U.S. HOUSEHOLDS ARE COSTCO MEMBERS

GLOBAL GROCERY SALES RANKINGS (U.S. GROCERS)[1]

($ in Billions) **National / Discount Grocers** | **Supermarket Grocers**

	#1	#2	#3	#4	#5	#6	#7	#8
	$404	$135	$129	$121	$121	$113	$85	$65
	Walmart / sam's club	COSTCO WHOLESALE	LIDL	ALDI [2] TRADER JOE'S	amazon WHOLE FOODS	Kroger	Ahold Delhaize	Albertsons Companies

Source: Company Filings & Company Websites as of September 2024.
1) Among grocers with operations in the U.S.
2) Includes Aldi Sud 2023 & Aldi Nord 2022 figures, which represents the latest publicly available information. Pro forma for Winn Dixie and Harveys stores recently acquired.

Roughly 40 percent of U.S. households are Costco members and roughly 54 percent of its U.S. sales comprise food and consumables, just in larger packs. As noted in a 2024 article entitled "How Costco Hacked the American Shopping Psyche," by *The New York Times*, **"They're selling the same food everyone else is selling."**[14]

The average U.S. Costco store generates roughly $300 million in revenue. At 54 percent grocery, that's $165 million of groceries per store, or $3 million in weekly grocery sales, which is three times the grocery sales of an exceptional supermarket (which generates ~$1 million per week) and five times that of the average supermarket (which generates ~$600 thousand per week).

I have given several speeches over the past few years at industry events and have often asked rooms full of hundreds of grocers to raise their hands if they

---

[14] https://www.nytimes.com/2024/08/20/dining/costco.html

have stores doing $3 million per week. There have never been any hands raised.

COSTCO'S EXTRAORDINARY GROCERY BUSINESS

GROCERY SALES ACCOUNT FOR 54% OF COSTCO'S ~$300M AVERAGE ANNUAL STORE REVENUE

AVERAGE GROCERY SALES PER STORE

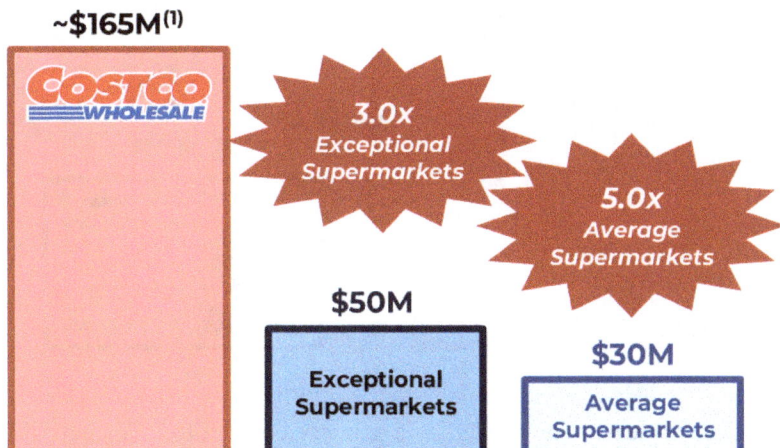

~$165M[1]

3.0x
Exceptional Supermarkets

5.0x
Average Supermarkets

$50M

Exceptional Supermarkets

$30M

Average Supermarkets

Source: Company filings and Capital IQ as of September 2024.
1)Costco food sales per store represents Food & Sundries and Fresh Food segments in U.S. stores.

As a result, Costco is the #3-ranked grocer in the United States. Its U.S. grocery sales are now $100 billion and have quadrupled in the past 20 years.

Then there's valuation. At $400 billion, Costco is currently worth more than twice as much as all public supermarkets and suppliers in the United States, *combined*. The market clearly thinks they're a good grocer.

COSTCO'S EXTRAORDINARY GROCERY BUSINESS DRIVING PREMIUM VALUATION

COSTCO'S VALUATION IS >2X MORE THAN ALL PUBLICLY-TRADED SUPERMARKETS AND SUPPLIERS, *COMBINED*

COSTCO'S FIRM VALUATION VS. ALL PUBLICLY-TRADED SUPERMARKETS

~$400B

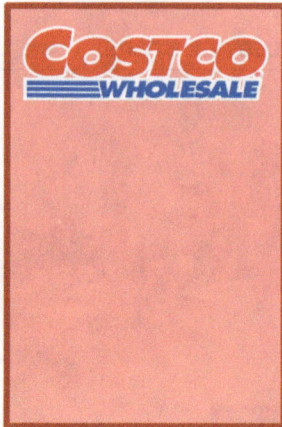

>2X
Above All Public Supermarkets / Suppliers Combined

~$190B

Source: Company filings and Capital IQ as of September 2024.

And Costco clearly views itself as a grocery competitor. Former CFO Rich Galanti said in Costco's December 2022 earnings call (before retiring), *"Our buyers are always looking at the supermarket ads, as well as the other warehouse club ads, what the pricing is, and we react to that."*

When Costco raised its membership fees in 2024, there was very little negative reaction, perhaps in part because at the same time the company announced it would raise wages for its teammates, who are already paid more than most in the industry. Having the financial capability to support employees — and getting credit with customers for doing so while raising prices on those customers — is a powerful combination.

Target

Target has evolved significantly since its founding as the Dayton Corporation in 1902. It used to own various department store chains, including Marshall Field's and Mervyn's.

After Walmart began to focus on grocery, Target followed suit in 1995 with its first SuperTarget store, which included a full grocery assortment. Target accelerated its transformation to becoming a bona fide grocer when it developed the PFresh store format in 2008 that included a significant grocery offering in Target stores.

Today, Target has nearly 2,000 stores across the United States, and most of the U.S. population lives within 10 miles of a Target store.

Over 50 percent of Target's $107 billion in sales are groceries. This is up 20 percent from 20 years ago, when groceries accounted for just 30 percent of Target's merchandise mix. As a result of this material shift, the company is now the #6 grocer in the United States, with a $55 billion grocery business that has grown over 400 percent in the past 20 years. The company employs 415,000 teammates, all non-union jobs.

TARGET HAS A $56 BILLION U.S. GROCERY BUSINESS, WITH OVER 400,000 NON-UNION JOBS

TARGET
Shipt

U.S. GROCERY SALES GROWTH

+5x

$56B

$11B

2003   2023

U.S. GROCERY JOBS GROWTH

+2x

415,000

245,000

2003   2023

Source: Company Filings & Company Websites as of September 2024.

In the past 20 years, Target has grown its store base by over 70 percent, adding over 700 stores and meaningfully increasing its concentration in some key population centers.

Target has also publicly announced its intention to grow its store base by another 300 stores in the next decade.[15]

---

[15] https://corporate.target.com/press/release/2024/03/target-announces-plans-to-deliver-enhanced-shopping-experience-in-2024-and-beyond

TARGET'S STORE BASE HAS GROWN OVER 50% SINCE 2003 AS ITS GROCERY BUSINESS CONTINUES TO EXPAND

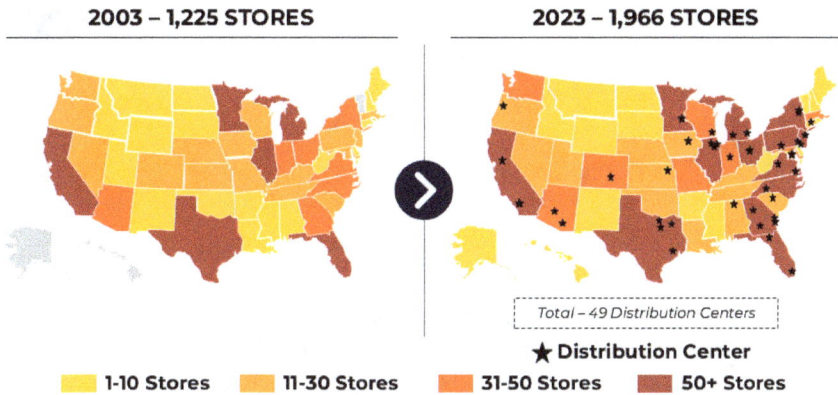

2003 – 1,225 STORES　　　**2023 – 1,966 STORES**

Total – 49 Distribution Centers

★ **Distribution Center**

| 1-10 Stores | 11-30 Stores | 31-50 Stores | 50+ Stores |

Target expects to open 20 new stores and add additional Ulta Beauty shop-in-shops during 2024

Source: Company filings and Company website.

Target's clear commitment to grocery leadership is evident in various comments from its leadership team.

In Target's March 2023 earnings call, Rick Gomez, currently Chief Commercial Officer, said,

> *Food and beverage has taken on a different role … over the last several years, we have been investing in the business…our food and beverage business has been growing … our fresh business is doing incredibly well. We've made big changes to specifications and quality control to deliver better, fresher product.*

And in the March 2024 earnings call, Gomez stated,

> *We have gone from being a retailer that just sells food to a retailer that truly celebrates food. And in doing that, we have made Target a destination for food.*

TARGET'S GROCERY BUSINESS HAS RADICALLY IMPROVED

Target has also become one of the biggest online grocers through Shipt, which the company acquired in 2017 for $550 million, enabling it to offer same-day grocery delivery in numerous markets across the country. Target does over $10 billion in online grocery sales and, through Shipt, fulfills orders for 200+ third-party retailers.

Aldi

Aldi is the world's #4 grocer and is #2 in Europe (Lidl is #3 in the world and #1 in Europe). Aldi has over 13,000 stores globally[16]. The company's owners, the Albrecht family in Germany, also own Trader Joe's. They are the 11th wealthiest family in the world.[17]

---

[16] Source: Aldi Sud 2023 & Aldi Nord 2022 Figures, which represent the latest publicly available information. Pro forma for Winn Dixie and Harveys stores acquired in 2024.

[17] https://www.thestreet.com/lifestyle/top-25-wealthiest-families-in-the-world-15072327#:~:text=11.,in%20U.S.%20grocer%20Trader%20Joe's.

ALDI IS THE #4 GLOBAL GROCER AND #2 IN EUROPE (LIDL IS #1)

GLOBAL GROCERY SALES RANKINGS (U.S. GROCERS)[1]

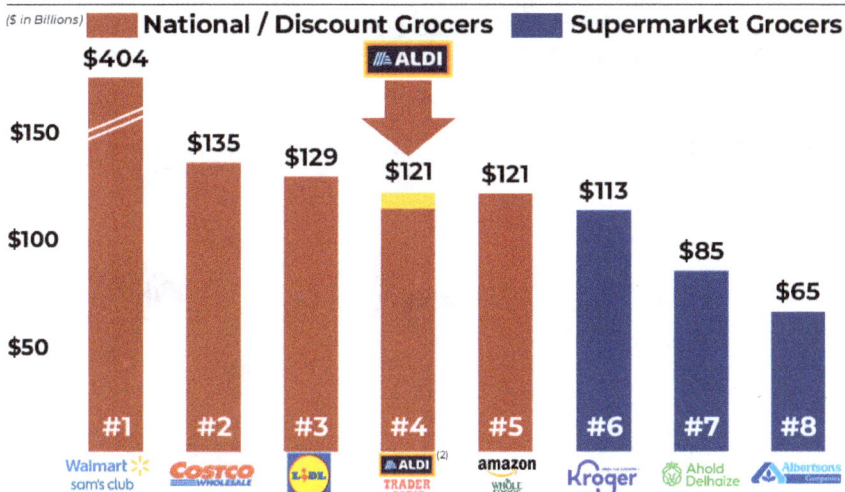

Source: Company Filings & Company Websites as of September 2024.
[1]Among grocers with operations in the U.S.
[2]Includes Aldi Sud 2023 & Aldi Nord 2022 figures, which represents the latest publicly available information. Pro forma for Winn Dixie and Harveys stores recently acquired.

Even in England, Aldi and its key German rival Lidl together have roughly 18 percent grocery share[18], having grown considerably since the 2008-2009 financial crisis. Aldi has a similar growth plan for the United States.

Aldi has grown from 680 U.S. grocery stores 20 years ago to over 2,800 today, including the 400 Winn Dixie stores Aldi recently acquired (which, given that most of those stores are expected to be converted to the Aldi format, may put an end to that storied grocer). For comparison, 2,800 stores are more than Kroger has today.

Aldi's CEO Jason Hart recently said on ABC News, *"A quarter of U.S. households now report that they shop at Aldi. That's twice what it was just*

---

[18] https://www.kantarworldpanel.com/grocery-market-share/great-britain/snapshot

six years ago."[19] He also recently said, ***"It's our goal to be America's first stop for grocery shopping…"***[20]

ALDI'S U.S. GROCERY BUSINESS HAS GROWN RAPIDLY, EVEN BEFORE ITS ACQUISITION OF WINN-DIXIE

ALDI'S U.S. STORE EXPANSION (2003 – 2023)

2003 – 680 STORES (24 STATES)

2023 – ~2,800 STORES (38 STATES)

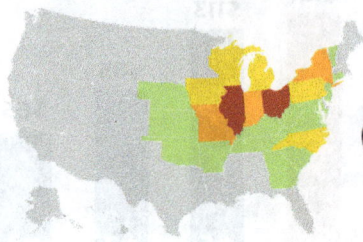

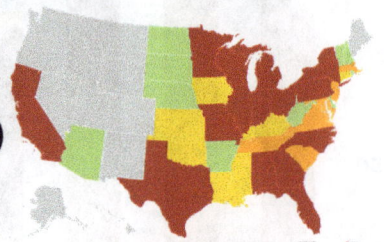

+4X Stores

1-20 Stores   21-49 Stores   50-74 Stores   75+ Stores

Source: Company Filings & Company Websites as of September 2024.

Aldi's U.S. sales have increased by 10x, from ~$3 billion to roughly $29 billion.[21] It has also added a lot of non-union jobs, from 7,000 teammates 20 years ago to over 85,000[22] estimated employees today.

That's what a huge global grocery business can do.

---

[19] https://abcnews.go.com/GMA/Food/aldi-stores-focusing-low-grocery-prices-summer-ceo/story?id=110496271

[20] https://progressivegrocer.com/friday-5-aldi-needs-suppliers-help-amazons-operational-kinks

[21] Source: The Progressive Grocer 100: Top Food Retailers in North America (May 2023 and 2024).

[22] Source: Forbes and https://sustainability.aldisouthgroup.com/about-aldi/national-markets

ALDI WILL HAVE A $29BN U.S. GROCERY BUSINESS WITH WINN-DIXIE, AND OVER 85,000 NON-UNION JOBS

U.S. GROCERY SALES GROWTH

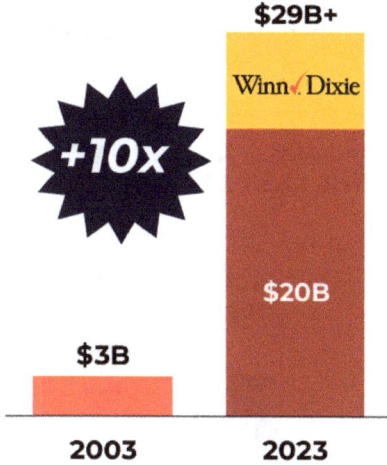

$29B+

Winn Dixie

+10x

$20B

$3B

2003   2023

U.S. GROCERY JOBS GROWTH

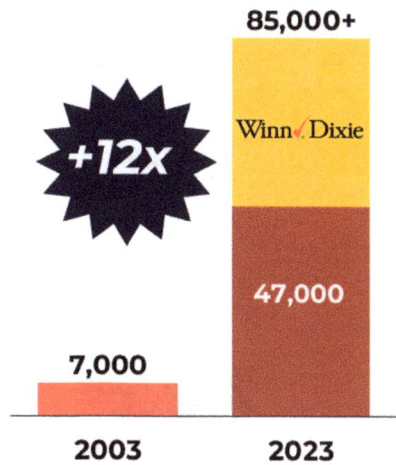

85,000+

Winn Dixie

+12x

47,000

7,000

2003   2023

Source: Company Filings & Company Websites as of September 2024.

Dollar General

Dollar grocers — and they are undeniably grocers — are the fastest-growing retail format, as well as the fastest-growing grocery format in the United States. Dollar grocers — particularly Dollar General and Family Dollar/Dollar Tree (which merged in 2015) — sell the same groceries as supermarket grocers, just in smaller packs. Grocery is the top category shopped in the dollar store sector.[23]

Dollar grocers are generally smaller than typical supermarket grocers and are mostly in suburban and more rural areas, but they have increasingly been opening stores in more heavily populated areas.

---

[23] ChaseDesign's 2023 Dollar Store Channel Survey https://progressivegrocer.com/are-dollar-stores-threat-traditional-supermarkets

Dollar grocers have significantly increased the share of grocery in their merchandise mix, with consumables now making up roughly 80 percent of sales at both Dollar General and Family Dollar. The chains have also added thousands of coolers and extensive fresh produce offerings. The broad customer acceptance of this evolution has only driven the dollar grocers to increase their investment in additional grocery stores over time.

DISCOUNT GROCERS HAVE TRANSFORMED AND SHIFTED THEIR FOCUS TO GROCERY OVER THE LAST 20 YEARS

DOLLAR GENERAL
GROCERY % OF REVENUE (2003 – 2023)

- 2003: 60%
- 2023: 82%
- +22%

DOLLAR TREE / FAMILY DOLLAR
GROCERY % OF REVENUE (2003 – 2023)

- 2003: 51% / 57%
- 2023: 63% / 81%
- +24%

Source: Company Filings & Company Websites as of September 2024.
Note: Grocery sales are defined as food & consumables as a percentage of total sales.

Dollar General has grown from 6,000 stores 20 years ago to over 20,000 today. The company has said publicly it has capacity for 34,000 stores in the United States; it opened over 2,800 stores from 2021 through 2023 (which, again, is more stores than Kroger has). In many southeastern markets, there is literally a Dollar General every three miles, in all directions. Dollar General stores seem to be everywhere in the Southeast and are multiplying rapidly across the country. The company's development and evolution to bona fide grocer over the past 20 years has been extraordinary.

DOLLAR GENERAL'S RAPID GROCERY GROWTH CONTINUES, WITH ~14,000 NEW STORES FROM 2003-2023 TO BECOME A NATIONAL GROCER

DOLLAR GENERAL

2003 – 6,113 STORES   **2023 – 20,345 STORES**

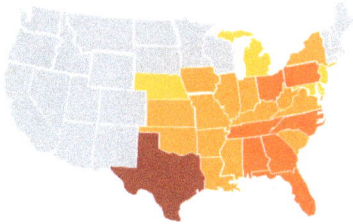

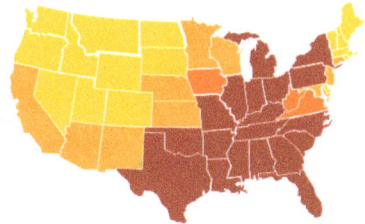

1-99 Stores   **100-299 Stores**   **300-499 Stores**   **500+ Stores**

Dollar General is projected to grow to 34,000 stores across the United States

Source: Company filings.
Note: Total Store Count represents latest available data as of September 2024.

Many people assume that the thrifty focus of dollar grocers suggests they only target customers at the lower end of the socioeconomic spectrum, but that is not accurate. In reality, the combination of the dollar grocers' ubiquity and consumers' trade-down response to inflationary pressures has given dollar grocers broad appeal across the income spectrum.

A recent *Wall Street Journal* article, "One-Percenters Keep Shopping at the Dollar Store," had a couple of quotes that really resonated with me:[24]

> *"No matter how much you make, there is no longer a stigma in going after a good deal."*

> *"A carrot is a carrot is a carrot."*

---

[24] https://www.wsj.com/articles/dollar-store-shoppers-wealthier-6e08ce1f

THE WALL STREET JOURNAL.

LIFE & STYLE

One-Percenters Keep Shopping at the Dollar Store

Wealthy consumers scour discount-chain aisles for bargains

June 19, 2023 9:00 pm ET

"No matter how much you make, there is no longer a stigma in going after a good deal."

"A carrot is a carrot is a carrot."

DOLLAR TREE

This broadening of consumer acceptance has enabled Dollar General to grow its grocery business at a very rapid clip.

Fresh grocery remains a key growth area for Dollar General. The company has been rapidly rolling out DG Fresh stores — which provide a variety of produce, refrigerated and frozen foods, fresh meat and dairy — to markets all over the United States.

DOLLAR STORES HAVE SIGNIFICANTLY EXPANDED THEIR GROCERY OFFERING

Source: Company Websites & Equity Research.

Katie Ellison, director of public relations at Dollar General, recently made the point very clearly in talking about the continued expansion of — and strong reception of — DG Fresh: *"People use it as a one-stop-shop for everything."*[25]

The recent press release in which Dollar General claimed it has *"more individual points of produce distribution than any other U.S. mass retailer or grocer"* — <u>over 5,000 stores</u> — was particularly striking to regional grocers across the country.

---

[25] https://progressivegrocer.com/how-dg-market-filling-fresh-food-gaps

Amid Dollar General's recently challenging operating dynamics while targeting customers at the lower end of the economic spectrum, CEO Todd Vasos confirmed the continued outperformance of grocery in the company's Q2 2024 earnings call:

> *Importantly, despite a weaker sales environment for our core customer than we had anticipated, we continue to grow market share in both dollars and units in highly consumable product sales.*[26]

While Dollar General is the largest dollar grocer, Family Dollar/Dollar Tree (officially, Dollar Tree, Inc.) is also extraordinarily large, with a roughly $19 billion grocery business in over 16,000 stores. The combined Family Dollar and Dollar Tree family has added over 9,000 stores, from under 7,000 stores

---

[26] https://www.grocerydive.com/news/dollar-general-and-dollar-tree-see-lackluster-q2-results-but-bright-spot-wi/726157/

in 2003 to over 16,000 stores in 2023. Combined grocery sales increased nearly 6 times, from $3 billion in 2003 to over $19 billion in 2023.

DOLLAR TREE / FAMILY DOLLAR ADDED ~10,000 NEW STORES FROM 2003 TO 2023 TO BECOME A NATIONAL GROCER

2003 – 6,879 STORES

2023 – 16,388 STORES

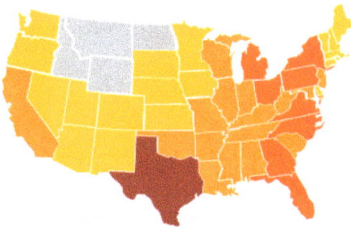

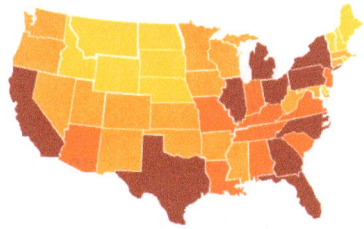

Legend: 1-99 Stores | 100-299 Stores | 300-499 Stores | 500+ Stores

Source: Company filings.
Note: Total Store Count represents latest available data as of September 2024.

In sum, Dollar General and Family Dollar/Dollar Tree together have more than 36,000 stores across the country and roughly $50 billion in U.S. grocery sales, up from roughly $7 billion 20 years ago — a 7 times increase. They also employ 395,000 people, all non-union jobs.

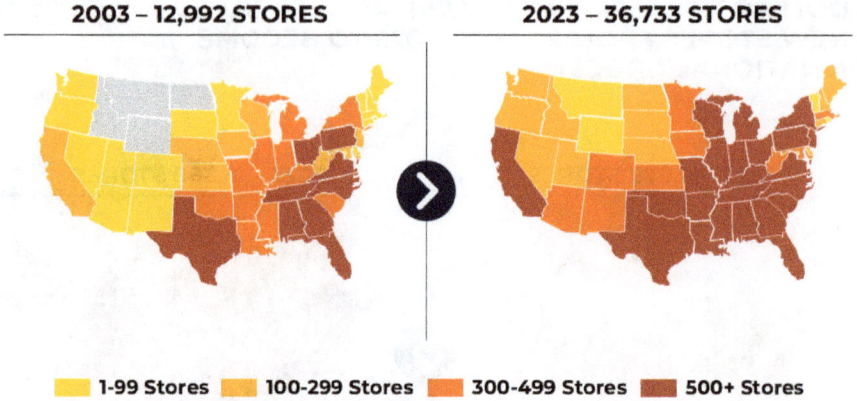

OVER THE PAST 20 YEARS, THE TWO LEADING DOLLAR GROCERS HAVE ADDED ~24,000 STORES & NOW GENERATE ~$50B IN ANNUAL GROCERY SALES

DOLLAR GENERAL
DOLLAR TREE
FAMILY DOLLAR

2003 – 12,992 STORES   **2023 – 36,733 STORES**

1-99 Stores   100-299 Stores   300-499 Stores   500+ Stores

~37,000 combined dollar grocery stores is well more than the <26,000 Supermarket Grocers remaining in the U.S.

Source: Company filings and Company Website.
Note: Total Store Count represents latest available data in Company's public filings / Store Locator.

Dollar General and Family Dollar/Dollar Tree have more stores in the United States than any other grocer, by a very wide margin.

DOLLAR AND NATIONAL / DISCOUNT GROCERS HAVE THE BENEFIT OF SCALE DUE TO RAPID STORE COUNT GROWTH

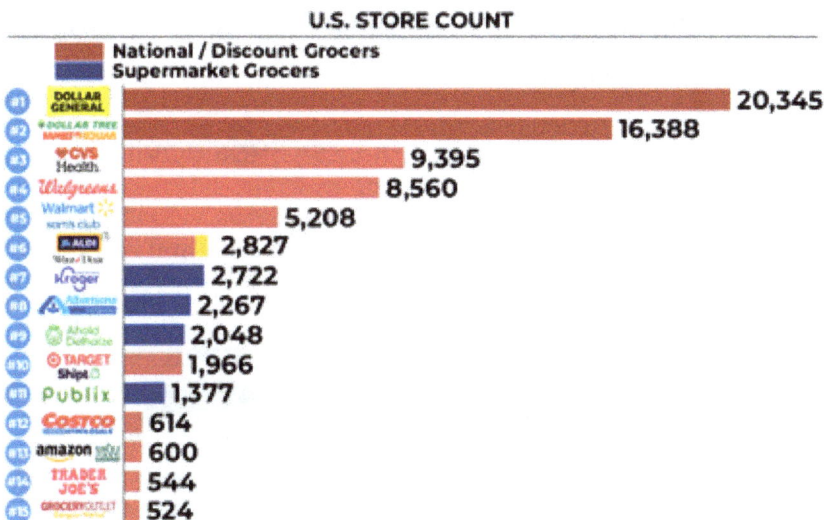

U.S. STORE COUNT

National / Discount Grocers
Supermarket Grocers

Rank	Retailer	Count
#1	DOLLAR GENERAL	20,345
#2	DOLLAR TREE FAMILY DOLLAR	16,388
#3	CVS Health	9,395
#4	Walgreens	8,560
#5	Walmart sam's club	5,208
#6	ALDI Winn-Dixie	2,827
#7	Kroger	2,722
#8	Albertsons	2,267
#9	Ahold Delhaize	2,048
#10	TARGET Shipt	1,966
#11	Publix	1,377
#12	Costco	614
#13	amazon	600
#14	TRADER JOE'S	544
#15	GROCERY OUTLET	524

Source: Company Filings & Company Websites as of September 2024.
1) Aldi figures include recent acquisition of Winn-Dixie and Harveys Stores.

Online Grocery

Online grocery has come a long way since Webvan and Kozmo in the late 1990s. While e-commerce profitability can be elusive, it is clear that larger baskets lead to more profitable deliveries.

When Walmart bought Jet.com in 2016, the gauntlet was thrown down in online grocery. Amazon responded by acquiring Whole Foods in 2017 and Target by buying Shipt later that year.

At the same time, Instacart was gaining steam as the go-to e-commerce partner for many grocers, from Costco to Family Dollar to Publix. In many ways, Instacart democratized online grocery access for regional grocers, but many struggled with the notion of ceding their most valuable asset, their relationships with their customers (generations-long relationships, in many cases), to a third party. Then Covid struck, and everything changed.

Covid drove online grocery to quadruple in the four years from 2018 to 2022. For many families, including mine, it was a lifeline. As noted earlier, we quite literally were able to survive Covid quarantine because of four different online grocers (all investment-grade credits).

ONLINE GROCERY HAS QUADRUPLED SINCE COVID

Source: FMI U.S. Grocery Shopper Trends: 2003, 2014, 2023, Progressive Grocer, Mercatus and Incisive Grocery.

Before Covid, 63 percent of Americans bought most grocery staples at physical stores; by 2023, it was down to 44 percent. Online grocery is used by 72 percent of U.S. households, over 50 percent of which purchase dairy, produce, meat and frozen groceries online. Only 36 percent of Millennials and 41 percent of Generation Z report buying groceries exclusively in a physical store.

Of shoppers who opt to purchase more grocery items through digital channels than brick-and-mortar grocery stores, 62 percent credit convenience while 54 percent cite lower price incentives and greater selection. Over 80 percent of grocery executives said that improving the integration between their brick-

and-mortar operations and digital systems is their top digital priority for 2024.[27]

Online grocery is projected to continue to grow rapidly in the next few years, to over $300 billion.

ONLINE GROCERY IS EXPECTED TO CONSISTENTLY INCREASE IN THE UPCOMING YEARS

Source: eMarketer and publicly available information as of September 2024. Adjusted to account for food and consumables sales.

Instacart's business grew so much during the pandemic that it was able to execute a big IPO in 2023. In its filings, Instacart disclosed that it reaches 95 percent of North American households. Its partners include over 1,400 retail banners and 80,000 stores. It serves millions of families every day.

These are the Instacart grocery choices in Seattle and Portland; the variety looks similar in most markets in the United States. Some markets have 10, 15, 20 or even 25 different grocers on the Instacart marketplace.

---

[27] Sources: Progressive Grocer, PYMNTS, Supermarket News, Mercatus and Incisive Grocery.

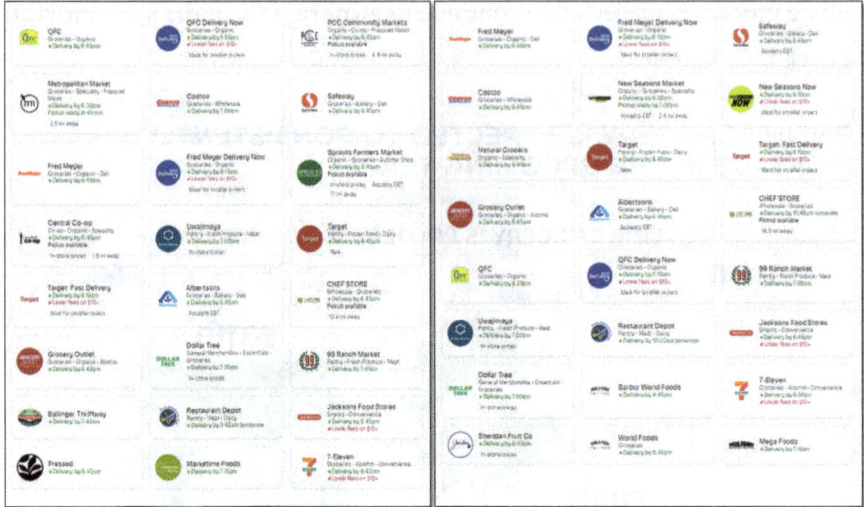

Source: Instacart Website.

Instacart has brought a truly unprecedented degree of grocery choice, convenience and price transparency across the country. From your sofa, your office, or basically anywhere, you can set up grocery delivery almost immediately. Whether on Instacart, or on white-label alternatives like Mercatus that many regional grocers use to maintain customer connectivity and data, it has simply never been easier for customers to check prices for items in their basket among an assortment of different grocers.

Even TikTok is exploring ways to become a grocery competitor. Mike Westgate, head of home, living and retail for TikTok Shop U.S., said that the platform is exploring partnerships that would enable it to distribute perishable groceries.[28]

---

[28] https://progressivegrocer.com/why-tiktok-another-retail-competitor

But the fact is, the highest-penetrated online grocers are not supermarket grocers — it's Walmart, Target, Costco and Amazon. According to Coresight, 68 percent of U.S. internet users who bought groceries online have purchased from Amazon; 65 percent purchased from Walmart; 28 percent purchased from Target; and 17 percent purchased from Costco. Aldi, Family Dollar, CVS, Walgreens and Rite Aid all use the same Instacart marketplace platform that dozens of regional grocers use.

AMAZON / WHOLE FOODS, WALMART, TARGET AND COSTCO DOMINATE ONLINE GROCERY

% OF ONLINE GROCERY PENETRATION

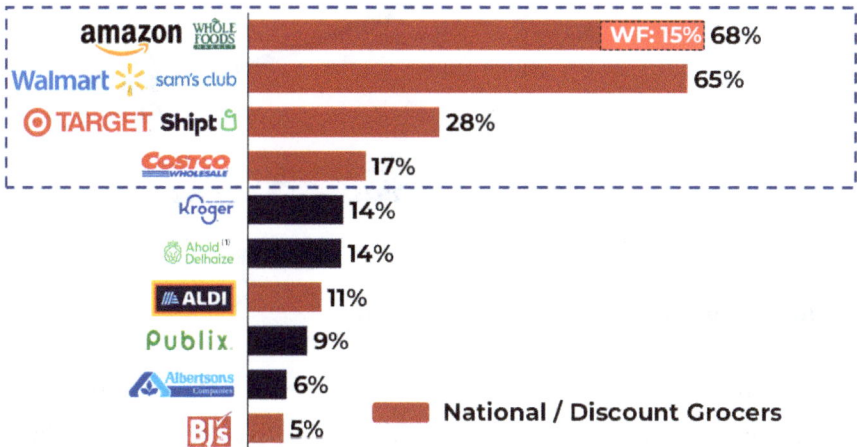

amazon WHOLE FOODS	WF: 15% 68%
Walmart sam's club	65%
TARGET Shipt	28%
Costco WHOLESALE	17%
Kroger	14%
Ahold[1] Delhaize	14%
ALDI	11%
Publix	9%
Albertsons Companies	6%
BJ's	5%

National / Discount Grocers

Source: Coresight Research.
1)Ahold Delhaize includes Fresh Direct and Peapod.

Grocery consultant Brick Meets Clicks, in a report with Mercatus, demonstrates that Walmart (even excluding Sam's club) captured 37 percent of the U.S. online grocery market in the second quarter of 2024, more than all supermarket grocers **combined**, which was only 27 percent. Three years ago, supermarket grocers accounted for 34 percent of online grocery; Walmart was just at 28 percent.[29]

WALMART (EXCL. SAM'S CLUB) CAPTURED 37% OF U.S. ONLINE GROCERY IN Q2 2024; MORE THAN ALL SUPERMARKETS COMBINED

U.S. E-GROCERY MARKET SHARE TRENDS: WALMART VS. SUPERMARKETS

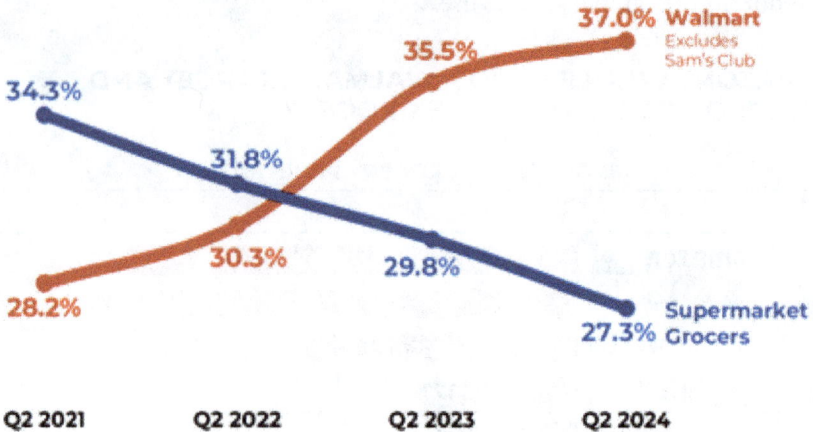

Source: Brick Meets Click/Mercatus Grocery Shopping Survey, 2021 - 2024

Walmart's Grocery Fulfillment Investment

The reason the enormous national/discount grocers are the most important online grocers comes back to cost of capital and credit ratings; Walmart Target, Costco and Amazon all have AA or A credit ratings. This gives them nearly unlimited capacity to invest in logistics and technology, well more than any supermarket.

Here's a clear manifestation: Walmart's ubiquitous fulfillment footprint. Walmart has over 200 fulfillment centers across the country.

---

[29] https://www.brickmeetsclick.com/presses/walmart-captures-a-record-37-of-u-s-egrocery-sales-in-q2-2024

WALMART'S EXTENSIVE FULFILLMENT FOOTPRINT IS UBIQUITOUS

Walmart

WALMART'S U.S. FULFILLMENT FOOTPRINT

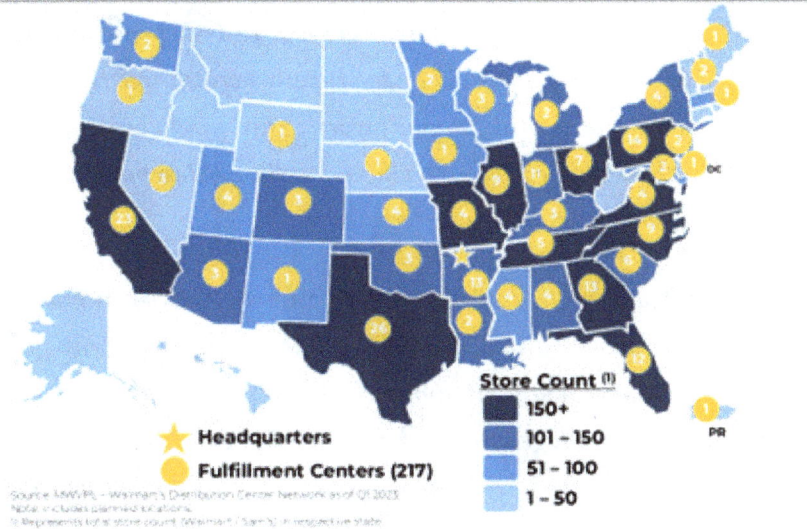

Source: MWPVL – Walmart's Distribution Center Network as of Q1 2023
Note: includes planned locations.
(1) Represents total store count (Walmart / Sam's) in respective state.

Headquarters

Fulfillment Centers (217)

Store Count (1)
- 150+
- 101 – 150
- 51 – 100
- 1 – 50

After spending countless billions developing fulfillment, Walmart has been making significant investments to optimize its portfolio with automation and robotics.

In 2022, Walmart acquired Alert Innovation, a robotics automation company that develops technology for automating order fulfillment in retail supply chains. Walmart had been working with Alert since 2016 on the development of its micro fulfillment centers (MFCs) to better leverage its store footprint for storage and fulfillment in order to better serve customers and pull further away from the competition. As described in an article on the company's website by Dave Guggina, the EVP of supply chain operations at Walmart U.S.:

For customers, this means orders can be fulfilled quickly and conveniently through pickup and delivery, giving them the items they want, when and where they want them. This system also enhances the experience for associates, who are integral to helping us perfect the system...

[F]ully autonomous bots...store, retrieve and dispense orders by moving horizontally, laterally and vertically across three temperature zones without any lifts or conveyors. This provides fewer space constraints inside the MFC and eliminates the need to pause the entire system for bot maintenance....

Bringing the best of Alert's technology and capabilities in-house will enable us to reach customers quicker by deploying MFCs with greater speed, providing both an unmatched shopping experience and a competitive advantage in omnichannel fulfillment. This is part of our broader goal to introduce the next generation of fulfillment centers and continue to transform our already world-class supply chain.[30]

Later in 2022, Walmart amplified its commitment to automation and robotics by expanding its relationship with Symbotic, an A.I.-powered supply chain technology company, announcing an agreement to implement Symbotic's robotics and software automation platform in all 42 of Walmart's regional distribution centers over time. Walmart also made a significant investment in Symbotic, amassing a significant ownership stake in the company, alongside Softbank and C&S owner Rick Cohen, who is also Symbotic's chairman, president and chief product officer.

The companies explained Symbotic's value proposition in their joint press release:

---

[30] https://corporate.walmart.com/news/2022/10/06/expanding-walmarts-market-fulfillment-center-capabilities-through-automation

The end-to-end software-enabled high-density robotics platform plays a strategic role in supporting [Walmart's] goal of modernizing its vast supply chain network and allows Walmart to transform its regional distribution centers to provide faster responsiveness to store orders, increased inventory accuracy and higher capacity for receiving and shipping freight to stores. The technology's ability to build palletized loads of department-sorted inventory ultimately enables Walmart to get products onto shelves...more quickly, while also making one of the toughest aspects of supply chain work — material handling — safer and simpler. It also creates new, tech-enabled jobs, such as cell operator and maintenance technician, that offer widely applicable skills in robotics and technology.[31]

Rick Cohen said the technology *"truly reinvent[s] the traditional warehouse and distribution of consumer goods across the supply chain."*[32]

Walmart continues to make extraordinary investments to modernize and automate its fulfillment network. As noted in another article by Walmart's Dave Guggina, the company continues to invest in order to enhance its customer relationships and solidify retention.

As customers change the way they shop, we're taking steps to build even more trust with them, ensuring the things they want — and need — are on shelves faster than ever before. To do that, we've been investing in data, increasingly intelligent software and automation — all to transform our business and create a more connected supply chain.[33]

---

[31] https://www.symbotic.com/about/news-events/news/walmart-and-symbotic-expand-partnership-to-implement-industry-leading-automation-system/
[32] Ibid.
[33] https://corporate.walmart.com/news/2024/07/10/walmarts-grocery-network-transformation-the-next-steps-on-our-supply-chain-modernization-journey

Walmart's latest perishables distribution center in Dallas can store twice the number of cases and process twice the volume of a traditional perishable facility, more than doubling the number of cases processed per hour.[34]

With this significant technological advantage (and extensive capacity to continue to invest behind it), Walmart continues to leverage its scale strength versus supermarket grocers to drive better prices.

According to Mercatus, assuming the same direct labor cost (though Walmart's is likely lower, given its non-union status), Walmart's fulfillment efficiencies, ad revenue and service fees lead to a net direct labor cost that is literally half that of supermarket grocers. As Walmart continues to implement robotics in its fulfillment centers, it expects to generate even more savings that can be used to further enhance technology and lower prices even more — which only strengthens its customer-loyalty-driven productivity loop.[35]

---

[34] Ibid.

[35] Mark Fairhurst, "Regional Grocers Will Face Tougher Fight Online Against Walmart." Mercatus, July 2023.

NATIONAL GROCERS' SCALE DRIVES STARK DIFFERENCE IN ONLINE GROCERY PROFITABILITY

ONLINE GROCERY ORDER-LEVEL ECONOMICS

	Supermarket Grocers	Walmart / sam's club
Direct Labor Cost	$13.70	$13.70
− Fulfillment Efficiencies	$2.40	$5.21
− Ad Revenue & Service Fees	$1.34	$3.60
= Net Direct Labor Cost	$9.96	$4.89

Walmart's net direct labor cost is 50% lower than that of Supermarket Grocers and is expected to grow to 60% by 2025E, driven by increased ad revenue

Source: Mercatus, "Regional Grocers Will Face Tougher Fight Online Against Walmart" July 2023

Walmart summarizes the effort very clearly:

> *Our business is growing. Walmart is the largest grocery retailer in the U.S., with our grocery network supporting over 4,600 stores with a massive pickup and delivery business that continues to grow as customers seek the convenience and value we offer.*[36]

You can't talk about Walmart's fulfillment investments and online grocery evolution without talking about its arch-rival, Amazon.

Amazon

Amazon's unique culture of experimentation has been the subject of numerous books and business articles. Jeff Bezos instilled the ethos of the company to

---

[36] https://corporate.walmart.com/news/2024/07/10/walmarts-grocery-network-transformation-the-next-steps-on-our-supply-chain-modernization-journey

always be "living in the future." To do that, he encouraged his team to iterate, learn, enhance and disrupt.

Amazon Prime started in 2005. Over time, it became clear the company recognized the brilliance (and extreme profitability) of Costco's membership subscription model. After evolving the Prime offering, Bezos was quoted as saying that he wanted it to be *"irresponsible to not have Prime."*[37]

A confluence of different factors made that the case for countless people. After Amazon followed Netflix into streaming, it began to invest in developing proprietary content that encouraged significant increases in Prime membership. For our family, it was the release of *The Marvelous Mrs. Maisel* in 2017. Once my wife heard about this show and was told *she **had** to see it*, we finally caved and got an Amazon Prime trial.

Like so many other Americans who get hooked on a show or two from different streaming platforms, we were locked in. We knew Amazon's prices were higher on most items if we ever needed to use Prime for delivery, but it was helpful to know we could get most items the next day, or sooner, if necessary. Like most Americans (including executives at many of Amazon's grocery rivals), we've since rationalized paying more on Amazon Prime for numerous products (far more often than I ever would have imagined) because of the time it saves us and how quickly we get the item.

Then Amazon had the same epiphany that Walmart had 30 years ago: *If you want to be the world's #1 Retailer, you need to be the #1 Grocer.* Acquiring Whole Foods in 2017 validated Amazon as a grocer and accelerated Prime's adoption across the country and the world.

The market loved the transaction so much that Amazon's equity value rose 2 percent that day, or $11 billion — almost enough to cover the $13.6 billion

---

[37] https://www.cnbc.com/video/2016/05/17/bezos-irresponsible-not-to-be-a-prime-member.html

acquisition cost. What was more telling, however, is what happened to the valuation of other grocers that day, and the value transfer that occurred. Kroger and Ahold Delhaize traded down 9 and 10 percent, respectively. Costco traded down 7 percent. Sprouts traded down 6 percent. Walmart and Target traded down 5 percent. In sum, for public grocers besides Amazon, it was a grocery industry bloodbath; they lost over $24 billion in value that day.

WHEN AMAZON ANNOUNCED ITS WHOLE FOODS ACQUISITION, ITS GROCERY PEERS SUFFERED HUGE VALUE LOSSES

WHILE AMAZON'S MARKET CAP INCREASED $11 BILLION, ITS GROCERY INDUSTRY PEERS LOST OVER $24 BILLION[1] IN VALUE

ONE-DAY % IMPACT ON MARKET VALUATION (JUNE 16, 2017)

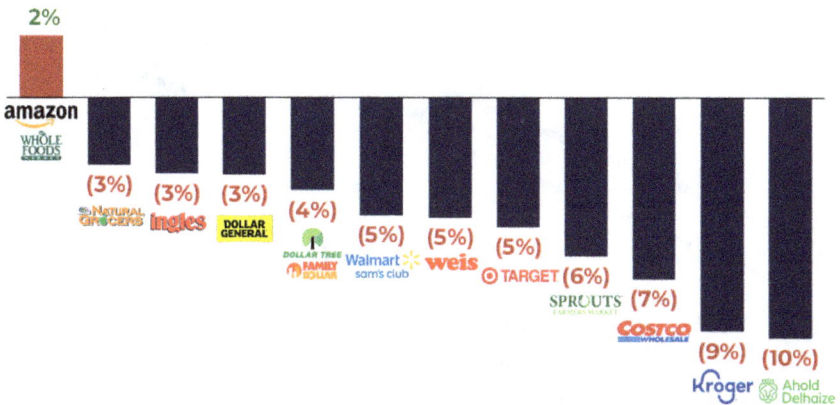

Source: Capital IQ and Company Filings.
1) Includes Ahold Delhaize, Costco, Dollar General, Dollar Tree / Family Dollar, Ingles, Kroger, Natural Grocers, SpartanNash, Sprouts, Target, UNFI, Walmart and Weis

There was significant overlap between Whole Foods and Amazon customers: 80 percent of Whole Foods customers were also Amazon customers; 60 percent were Prime Members. At the time, roughly 70 percent of the U.S. population lived within 10 miles of a Whole Foods, which provided $16 billion in grocery sales and 460 stores that could serve as small, refrigerated distribution centers for Prime and Amazon Fresh.

Today, over 60 percent of U.S. consumers are Amazon Prime members.[38]

At the end of 2023, Amazon's ecosystem had over 230 million Prime members worldwide, up from 20 million ten years prior, a 28 percent annual growth rate. With a $139 per year subscription fee, Amazon earns roughly $32 billion in cash from Prime before it even sells anything!

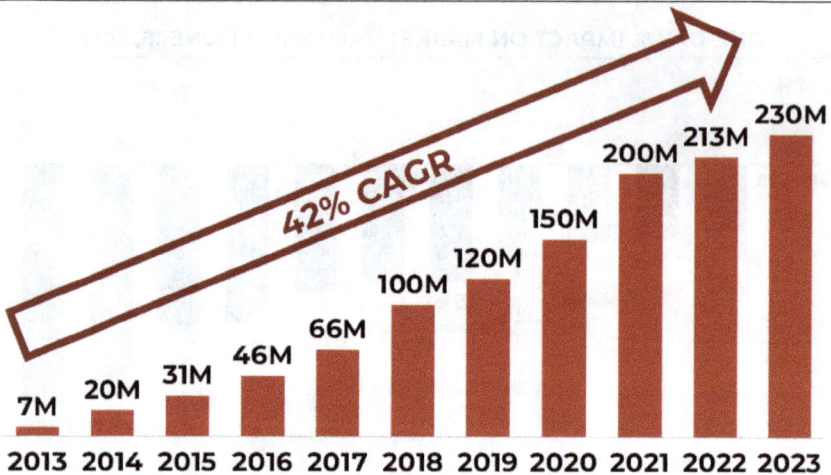

AMAZON CONTINUES TO GAIN STRENGTH WITH PRIME MEMBERSHIP INCREASES

AMAZON HAS RAPIDLY GROWN ITS PRIME MEMBER BASE

GLOBAL AMAZON PRIME MEMBERS (2013-2023)

42% CAGR

Source: eMarketer, Business of Apps, Yaguara.co and publicly available information.

Add on Amazon's roughly $50 billion advertising business, and that's over $80 billion in cash, each year — and it's growing, fast.

PRIME MEMBERSHIP FEES AND ADVERTISING REVENUE amazon
PROVIDE AMAZON WITH EXTRAORDINARY CASH FLOW

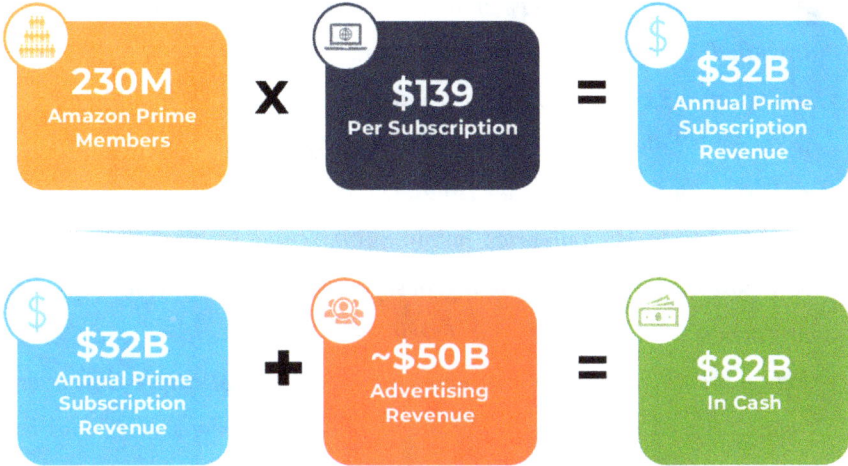

230M
Amazon Prime
Members

X

$139
Per Subscription

=

$32B
Annual Prime
Subscription
Revenue

$32B
Annual Prime
Subscription
Revenue

+

~$50B
Advertising
Revenue

=

$82B
In Cash

Amazon's Prime Day has become a national sale day that drives an extraordinary amount of revenue, particularly in grocery. In July 2024, Prime Day was estimated to have generated over $14 billion in sales.[39] According to a survey by Numerator, more than half of shoppers said they were waiting for Prime Day to purchase a product they intended to buy. In addition to securing great deals on TVs, iPads and housewares, 13 percent of shoppers said they also bought groceries, and 35 percent said they price-checked against both Walmart and Target for better prices before purchasing their items.[40]

As striking as those figures are, what's arguably even more stunning is the customer loyalty and demand elasticity Amazon has developed with Prime, notwithstanding significant price increases for the service. As leading

---

[39] https://techcrunch.com/2024/07/18/amazon-prime-day-2024-sales-hit-record-14-2-billion/
[40] https://www.numerator.com/press/amazon-prime-day-2024-early-results-are-in-numerator-reports/

industry journalist (and good friend) Kevin Coupe pointed out in late 2023, when there was yet another material price increase:

> *At the beginning of 2021, Prime, which cost $119 a year at the time, included unlimited Whole Foods and Amazon Fresh deliveries on orders over $35 at no extra cost. Later that year, Amazon added a $10 fee to all Whole Foods deliveries. In 2022, Amazon jacked the total price of Prime up to $139. Earlier [in 2023], it started charging fees of up to $10 on all Fresh deliveries below $100. Then [in December 2023], Amazon said it was piloting a grocery-delivery subscription that offers unlimited Whole Foods and Fresh deliveries on orders over $35 to Prime members who pay an extra $10 a month. Multiply that over a year and add it to the base Prime fee, and the same service that cost $119 in 2021 now costs a whopping $259.*[41]

That's pricing power.

With the combination of these dynamics, along with its leading AWS global cloud services business, Amazon's EBITDA has tripled since early 2020, increasing over $69 billion from $34 billion to $104 billion. By comparison, Walmart's EBITDA is $41 billion; Costco's EBITDA is $11 billion; in other words, Amazon's four-year EBITDA *increase* is more than Walmart and Costco's total EBITDA *combined,* and over six times Costco's (and they both have grown their EBITDA significantly).

---

[41] https://morningnewsbeat.com/2023/12/08/amazon-pilots-new-grocery-delivery-subscription-program/

AMAZON'S EBITDA GROWTH FAR ECLIPSES ITS GROCERY PEERS

amazon

AMAZON'S EBITDA HAS NEARLY TRIPLED SINCE EARLY 2020, FROM $34 BILLION TO OVER $100 BILLION

CURRENT EBITDA AND EBITDA GROWTH SINCE JANUARY 2020

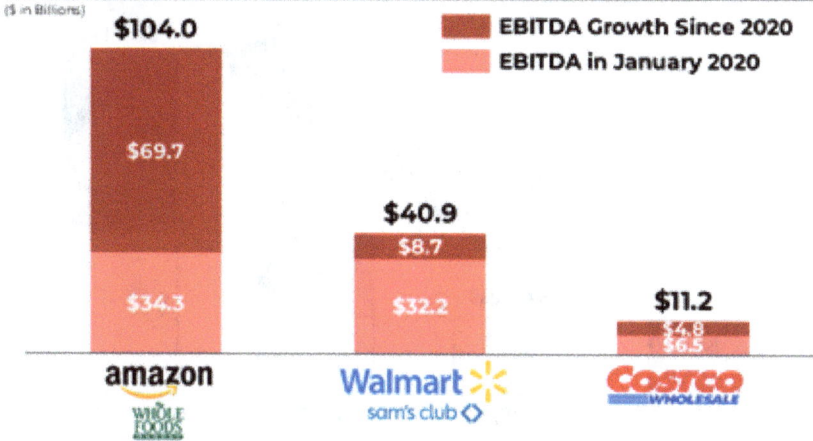

($ in Billions)

- EBITDA Growth Since 2020
- EBITDA in January 2020

$104.0
- $69.7
- $34.3

amazon
WHOLE FOODS

$40.9
- $8.7
- $32.2

Walmart
sam's club

$11.2
- $4.8
- $6.5

COSTCO
WHOLESALE

Source: CapIQ as of September 2024

Amazon was worth (only) $461 billion when it announced its Whole Foods acquisition in 2017. Its value doubled by early 2020, before Covid; it has doubled again to **_$2 trillion_** since January 2020, increasing $1 **_trillion_** since then and $1.6 **_trillion_** since Whole Foods.

SINCE AMAZON ANNOUNCED WHOLE FOODS IN JUNE 2017, IT HAS GAINED OVER $1.6 TRILLION IN VALUE amazon

WHOLE FOODS

AMAZON'S VALUATION OVER TIME

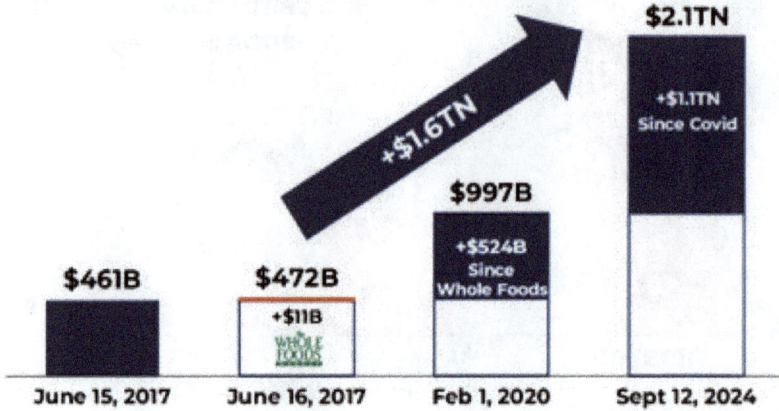

$2.1TN

+$1.1TN
Since Covid

+$1.6TN

$997B

+$524B
Since
Whole Foods

$461B

$472B

+$11B
WHOLE FOODS

June 15, 2017   June 16, 2017   Feb 1, 2020   Sept 12, 2024

Source: Capital IQ and Company filings as of September 2024.
Note: Valuation refers to Enterprise Value (Equity Value + Net Debt)

In 2023 alone, Amazon's value increased over $800 billion. That's more than Walmart's $690 billion current market valuation as of this writing. It's 10 times the current value of Kroger and Albertsons, **combined**.

In fact, Amazon is worth more than all U.S. grocers, **combined,** by a lot (nearly 40 percent more than Walmart, Target, Costco, CVS, Walgreens, Dollar General, Family Dollar/Dollar Tree, Kroger, Ahold Delhaize, Albertsons, etc.).

AMAZON'S $2.1 TRILLION VALUATION EXCEEDS ALL OTHER PUBLICLY-TRADED U.S. GROCERS, COMBINED

AMAZON'S FIRM VALUATION VS. ALL PUBLICLY-TRADED U.S. GROCERS

($ in Trillions)

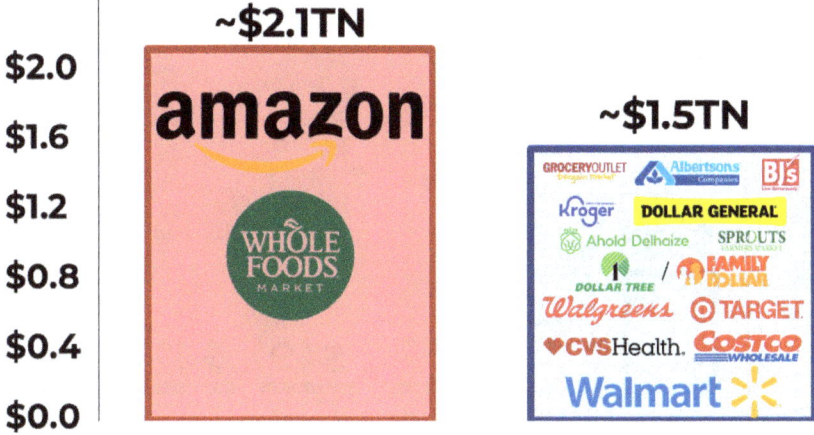

Source: Company filings and Capital IQ as of September 2024.
Note: All Other Public-Traded U.S. Grocers includes Ingles, Weis, Village, Natural Grocers, SpartanNash and United Natural Foods.

Amazon's valuation is literally three times Walmart's valuation; five times Costco; 40 times Publix; 43 times Kroger, 44 times Ahold Delhaize and over 110 times the valuation of Albertsons.

AMAZON'S $2.1 TRILLION VALUATION IS MANY MULTIPLES ITS GROCERY COMPETITORS

amazon

($ In Billions)

WHOLE FOODS

AMAZON'S FIRM VALUATION AND MULTIPLES OF COMPETITORS

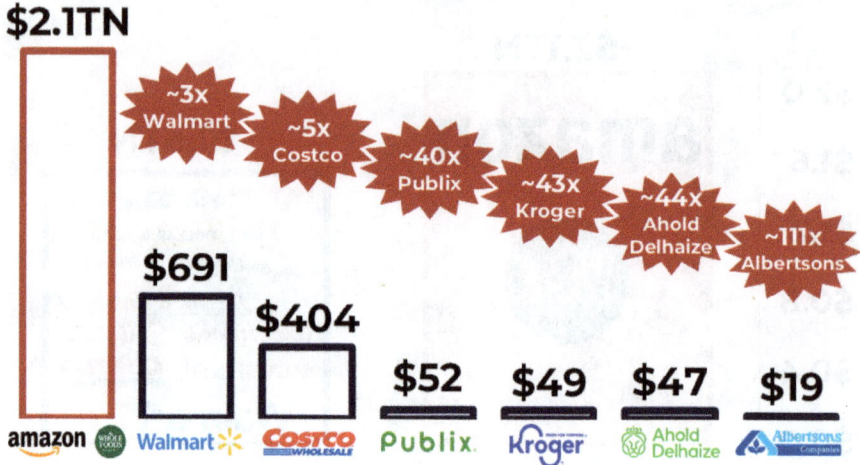

$2.1TN

~3x Walmart
~5x Costco
~40x Publix
~43x Kroger
~44x Ahold Delhaize
~111x Albertsons

$691 $404 $52 $49 $47 $19

amazon | Walmart | COSTCO WHOLESALE | Publix | Kroger | Ahold Delhaize | Albertsons Companies

Source: Company filings and Capital IQ as of September 2024.

Valuation is important because, coupled with its extraordinary market value, Amazon is also an AA credit, which, as noted above, means it borrows cheaper than most countries. Amazon's very low cost of capital and extremely high equity valuation give it a near-limitless ability to invest in the Prime ecosystem that competes with all grocers, but particularly supermarket grocers. The effect of these investments is cumulative and geometric.

When Amazon started spending $1 billion per quarter on next-day delivery in 2019,[42] it only cost them 6 basis points of its market value (0.06 percent) at the time. Those deliveries may be profitable, they may not be. But while it barely moves the cost needle for Amazon, it meaningfully changes the game and raises the bar — and costs in the arms race for customer acquisition and retention — for everyone else.

---

[42] https://www.geekwire.com/2019/amazon-will-spend-nearly-1-5b-q4-one-day-delivery-initiative-shipping-costs-skyrocket/

When Amazon acquired PillPack for $744 million in 2018 to get into the prescription drug business, it cost just a few basis points of valuation. But look at the impact the acquisition had on drug retail valuations: each of CVS, Walgreens and Rite Aid had significant declines the following day.

MARKET REACTION TO AMAZON'S ACQUISITION OF PILLPACK

RITE AID, WALGREENS AND CVS, THE THREE BIGGEST PHARMACY PLAYERS, HAD LARGE VALUATION DECLINES FOLLOWING AMAZON'S ACQUISITION OF PILL PACK

ONE-DAY % IMPACT ON MARKET VALUATION (JUNE 26, 2018 TO JUNE 27, 2018)

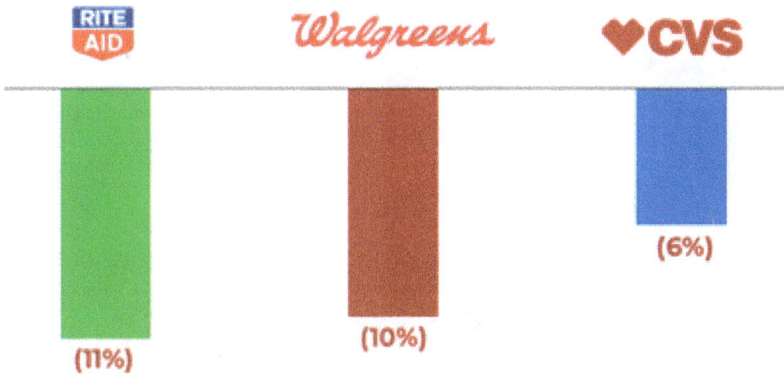

Source: Capital IQ and Company Filings

Amazon's $8 billion acquisition of MGM in 2022 cost ~0.51 percent of Amazon's value at the time; but it added *James Bond* and *Rocky* movies (among countless others) to join *Mrs. Maisel* in making Prime Video even more attractive for member subscribers, who in turn buy more goods and more groceries, more often, from Amazon.

Beyond Amazon's enormous online grocery business, turbo-charged through Prime as it is, the company has developed a variety of different grocery and pharmacy formats, from Whole Foods and Amazon Fresh to the PillPack acquisition. It also acquired primary health care company One Medical, which has over 220 offices in 27 markets across the country, for $3.9 billion.

While all of these formats are progressing at varying cadences, they all are undeniably having a material impact on the market broadly, particularly grocery and pharmacy competitors.

AMAZON'S LARGE GROCERY BUSINESS SERVES CONSUMERS ACROSS THE U.S. WITH VARIOUS FORMATS

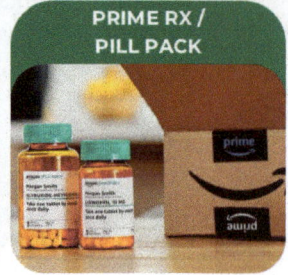

Andy Jassy conceded in his April 2023 earnings call that the company still has work to do with Amazon Fresh:

> *And if you really want to serve as much of grocery as we'd like to, you have to have a mass physical offering. And that's what we've been working on for a few years with a brand we've called Amazon Fresh. We wish we were further along at this point. We've tried lots of ideas. We haven't yet found conviction around the format that we want to go expand much more broadly. We have a set of experiments and ideas and concepts that we're working on across our dozens of stores there. And we're pretty optimistic that we have something that may very well work. ...we continue to believe it's a big business for us today. It's*

continuing to get bigger, but we believe we have the opportunity for it to be much larger for Amazon and where we can help customers more broadly. And I think having that physical presence, we will also have the ability both to be able to serve the grocery products they come for as well as store some other pieces and help customers across some other product lines as well.

In the summer of 2024, Amazon opened four high-tech Amazon Fresh grocery stores and invited customers to experience grocery shopping with Amazon Fresh, both in-store and online:

We're excited for customers to see our wide selection of grocery essentials from national brands, high-quality produce, meat and seafood, and curated array of their favorite local items and fresh-prepared meals.[43]

Customers can save up to 30 percent on 4,000 weekly rotating grocery items, both in-store and online, every day. Prime members have exclusive access to Prime Savings, which offers a 10 percent discount on hundreds of additional grocery items across the aisles.[44]

As Walmart has significantly increased its capital allocation to technology and fulfillment, Amazon has not been outdone. While continuing to experiment with different formats like Amazon Fresh with which to serve customers, the company has made a steady stream of significant capital investments in distribution, fulfillment logistics, automation and AI.

Amazon is leveraging an $80 billion annual technology and infrastructure budget that only costs a small percentage of its value. It has quietly built an

---

[43] https://chainstoreage.com/amazon-opens-four-high-tech-grocery-stores
[44] Ibid.

enormous network of over 400 fulfillment centers and over 1,000 hubs and sorting facilities.

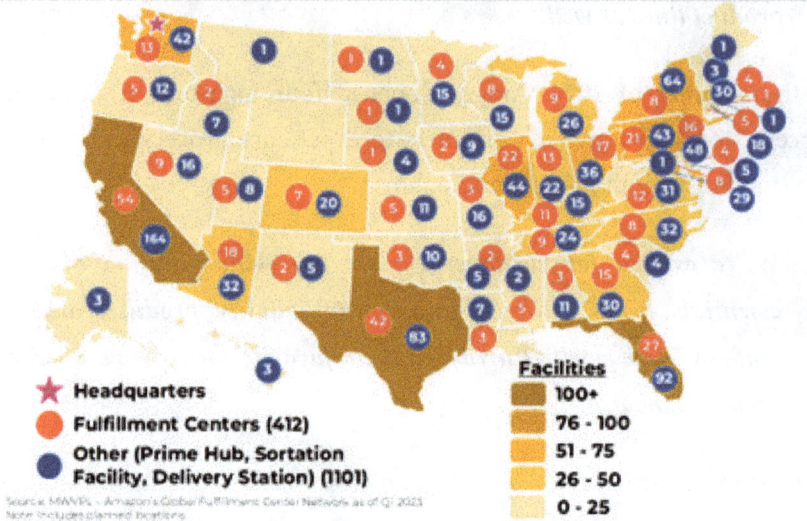

AMAZON'S EXTRAORDINARY FULFILLMENT FOOTPRINT IS UBIQUITOUS

amazon

AMAZON'S U.S. FULFILLMENT FOOTPRINT

★ Headquarters
● Fulfillment Centers (412)
● Other (Prime Hub, Sortation Facility, Delivery Station) (1101)

Source: MWPVL - Amazon's Global Fulfillment Center Network as of Q1 2023
Note: Includes planned locations

Facilities
100+
76 - 100
51 - 75
26 - 50
0 - 25

Amazon now has 440 million square feet of fulfillment capacity, up from roughly 100 million square feet just eight years ago.

AMAZON HAS BUILT SIGNIFICANT FULFILLMENT CAPABILITIES IN THE PAST 15 YEARS

amazon

AMAZON'S FULFILLMENT CENTERS SQUARE FOOTAGE

(Sq. Ft. in Millions)

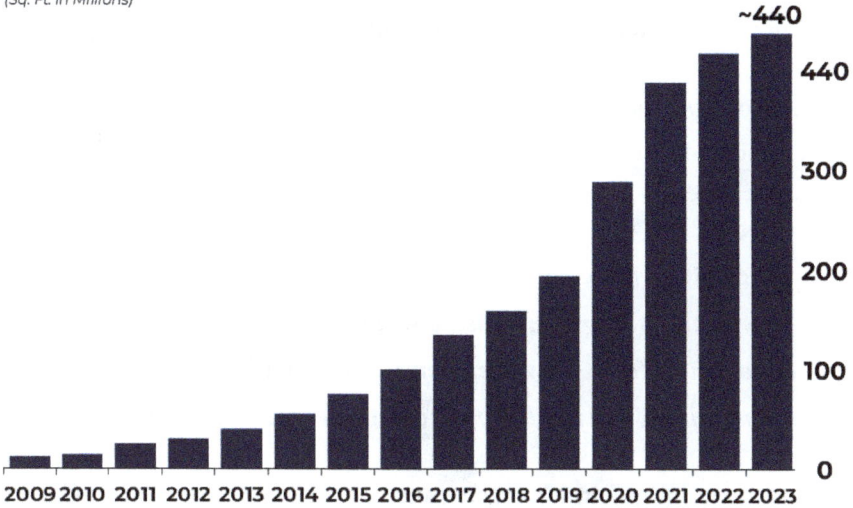

Source: UBS U.S. Retail Research as of April 2024.

Amazon is driving process improvements with robotics and automated fulfillment to lower service costs and accelerate delivery times. In an October 2023 article by Scott Dresser, Amazon's VP of Robotics (yes, Amazon has a VP of Robotics), the company expounded on the various ways it is using robots to support employees and speed up customer delivery times.

We now have over 750,000 robots working collaboratively with our employees, taking on highly repetitive tasks and freeing employees up to better deliver for our customers...

[The] Sequoia [robotic system] will help us delight customers with greater speed and increased accuracy for delivery estimates, while also improving employee safety at our facilities. Sequoia allows us to identify and store inventory we receive at our fulfillment centers up to 75 percent faster than we can today. This means we can list items for sale on Amazon.com more quickly, benefiting both sellers and

customers. When orders are placed, Sequoia also reduces the time it takes to process an order through a fulfillment center by up to 25 percent, which improves our shipping predictability and increases the number of goods we can offer for Same-Day or Next-Day shipping.[45]

In Amazon's April 2024 earnings call, CEO Andy Jassy reiterated the clear importance of grocery and logistics efficiency to Amazon's long-term strategy:

We continue to be optimistic about what we're doing in grocery. We have a very large grocery business...Faster delivery times have another important effect. As we get items to customers this fast, customers choose Amazon to fulfill their shopping needs more frequently.

That same month, Tony Hoggett, Amazon's SVP of Worldwide Grocery Stores, said:

Our goal is to build a best-in-class grocery shopping experience — whether shopping in-store or online — where Amazon is the first choice for selection, value and convenience.[46]

In July 2024, to support its omnichannel offering with AI efficiency, Amazon made Rufus, its generative AI-powered conversational shopping assistant, available to all Amazon customers on its app. As Amazon put it in an article on its website, *"it's like having a shopping assistant with you any time you're in our store."*[47]

---

[45] https://www.aboutamazon.com/news/operations/amazon-introduces-new-robotics-solutions
[46] https://progressivegrocer.com/amazon-introduces-low-cost-grocery-delivery
[47] https://www.aboutamazon.com/news/retail/how-to-use-amazon-rufus

Amazon also announced in a July 2024 press release that it had set a new record, delivering more than five billion items globally the same or next day, a 30 percent increase over the prior year:

> *Tens of millions of our most popular items are available with free Same-Day or One-Day Delivery, which means Prime today offers 20 times more selection that can be delivered twice as fast as when Prime first launched.*
>
> *...In the U.S., Amazon offers more than 300 million items with free Prime shipping compared to one million when the membership program launched in 2005.*[48]

Amazon accomplished this by expanding its same-day network, regionalizing its fulfillment network to shorten delivery distances, and using AI algorithms to predict demand and optimize inventory management.

This is just a subset of all the different ongoing initiatives Amazon is employing to overtake Walmart as the world's leading retailer. There will continue to be collateral damage.

Consequently, what is fascinating for retail observers — and perhaps most disconcerting for its grocery peers — is that by Jassy's own admission, Amazon has not yet "figured out" grocery.

So, given Amazon's unmatched financial resources and crystal-clear commitment to grocery as part of its ubiquitous global retail leadership (domination) strategy, the daunting question pervading American grocery boardrooms is, **What happens when they do?**

---

[48] https://www.aboutamazon.com/news/retail/amazon-prime-same-day-delivery-speed-2024

CHAPTER 3

Financial Consequences
for Supermarket Grocers

By now, it should be fairly clear that the national/discount grocers have grown a lot over the last 20 years. Most people don't appreciate just how much.

Walmart's U.S. grocery business has grown by over $250 billion; Costco's U.S. grocery business is up $80 billion; Amazon/Whole Foods' U.S. grocery business is up over $60 billion; Target/Shipt is up over $40 billion; and the dollar grocers are up over $40 billion.

NATIONAL / DISCOUNT GROCERS HAVE ADDED EXTRAORDINARY AMOUNTS OF GROCERY SALES IN THE PAST 20 YEARS

20-YEAR U.S. GROCERY SALES GROWTH (TOP 15 GROCERS)

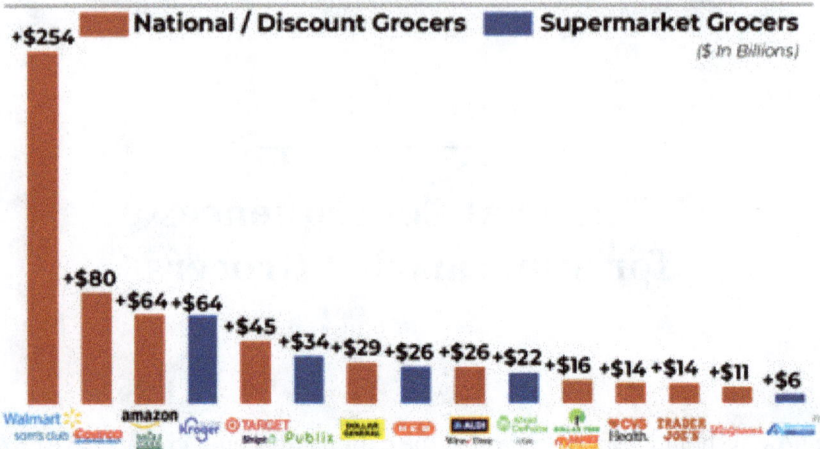

This becomes even more stark when looking at the 20-year sales change in percentage terms. Amazon's U.S. grocery business is up 2500 percent; Aldi's up over 900 percent; Dollar General is up nearly 800 percent; Trader Joe's is up over 600 percent; Costco and Target are each up roughly 400 percent. The top eight grocery growth companies are all national/discount grocers, all ahead of HEB and Publix.

NATIONAL / DISCOUNT GROCERS HAVE INCREASED GROCERY SALES RAPIDLY IN THE PAST 20 YEARS

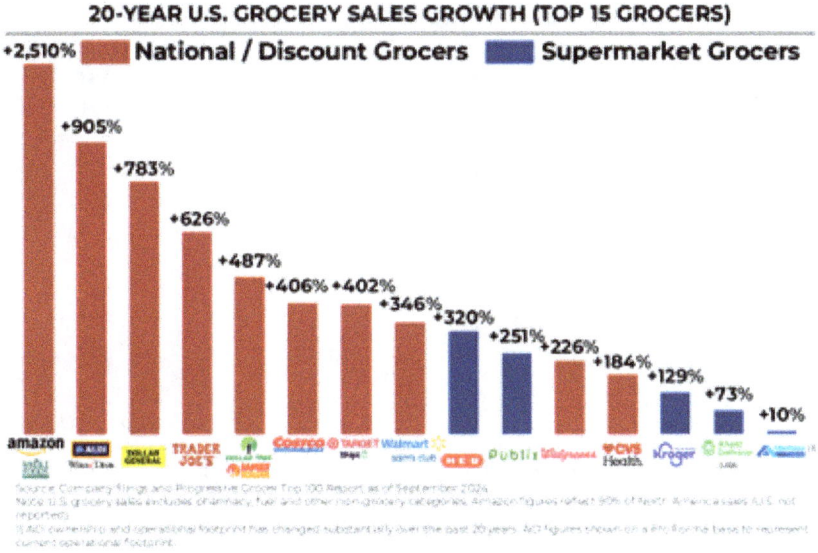

20-YEAR U.S. GROCERY SALES GROWTH (TOP 15 GROCERS)

National / Discount Grocers Supermarket Grocers

+2,510%
+905%
+783%
+626%
+487%
+406% +402%
+346% +320%
+251% +226%
+184% +129%
+73% +10%

Source: Company filings and Progressive Grocer Top 100 Report, as of September 2024.
Note: U.S. grocery sales excludes pharmacy, fuel and other non-grocery categories. Amazon figures reflect 90% of North America sales (U.S. not reported).
*(ALDI ownership and operational footprint has changed substantially over the past 20 years. ALDI figures shown on a Pro Forma basis to represent current operational footprint.)

When you add it all up, the national/discount grocers have added over $500 billion in grocery sales. ***That's a half-<u>trillion</u> dollars.*** This accounts for the vast majority of growth in the grocery industry.

The national/discount grocers have added over 39,000 new grocery stores, which is nearly ***90x more store growth*** than supermarket grocers have achieved.

NATIONAL / DISCOUNT GROCERS GROWTH HAS FAR EXCEEDED THAT OF SUPERMARKET GROCERS OVER THE PAST 20 YEARS

GROCERY GROWTH (2003 – 2023, TOP 15 GROCERS)

GROCERY SALES GROWTH	STORE COUNT GROWTH
($ In Billions)	

GROCERY SALES GROWTH
- +$552 / +420%
- 3.7x
- +$151 / +95%
- Supermarket Grocers
- National / Discount Grocers

STORE COUNT GROWTH
- +39,775 / +148%
- 88.8x
- +448 +5%
- Supermarket Grocers
- National / Discount Grocers

Source: Company filings and Progressive Grocer Top 100 Report as of September 2024.
Note: Represents top 15 national / discount and supermarket grocers, which includes Walmart, Kroger, Costco, Albertsons, Amazon, Target, Ahold Delhaize, Publix, H-E-B, Walgreens, Dollar General, CVS, Aldi, Dollar Tree / Family Dollar and Trader Joe's.

This radical difference in sales and store growth vis-à-vis the national/discount grocers has resulted in considerable financial consequences for supermarket grocers.

When evaluating the strength of different companies, many people focus on sales, but from a financial perspective that's not the whole story: Sears and Kmart had lots of sales; then they didn't. While a company's sales level has a substantial impact on its credit rating, as noted earlier, EBITDA — cash flow — and valuation drive liquidity, which in turn drives capacity to acquire and retain customers. That's retail (and grocery) oxygen.

There is a vast EBITDA difference between Amazon, Walmart and Costco versus everyone else.

While Amazon's EBITDA is literally 2.5 times that of Walmart and 9 times that of Costco, it is nearly 13 times Kroger's EBITDA, which ranks just #6 among U.S. grocers. While much of Amazon's EBITDA growth is driven by

AWS and other business lines, this does not change the impact on its capacity to usurp grocery market share at will.

THERE IS AN EXTREME EBITDA DIFFERENCE BETWEEN AMERICA'S NATIONAL / DISCOUNT GROCERS AND THEIR SUPERMARKET GROCER PEERS

($ in Billions)

LTM EBITDA

Source: Capital IQ and Company Filings as of September 2024

What is perhaps more staggering is the extent to which some of the national/discount grocers increased their EBITDA during the pandemic. Amazon's growth is more than all the public grocers **combined**. It so significant we have to break the y axis of the chart to fit it all on a legible chart. Amazon's EBITDA is currently $69.7 billion higher than it was pre-pandemic; Walmart's EBITDA is $8.7 billion higher. Notably, Costco's EBITDA, driven by its spectacular success investing in its grocery operations, both in-store and online, has increased $4.8 billion.

While many grocers experienced EBITDA increases during Covid, most regional operators have since ceded much, if not all, of those gains. The growth at Amazon, Walmart and Costco plainly dwarfs the rest of the sector. The clear implication is that during the pandemic, the national/discount grocers meaningfully enhanced their competitive position over smaller supermarket grocers, who, unfortunately, are arguably far further behind on a relative basis than they were before Covid.

LARGER OPERATORS, PARTICULARLY AMAZON, GENERATED EXTRAORDINARY EBITDA GROWTH SINCE THE PANDEMIC

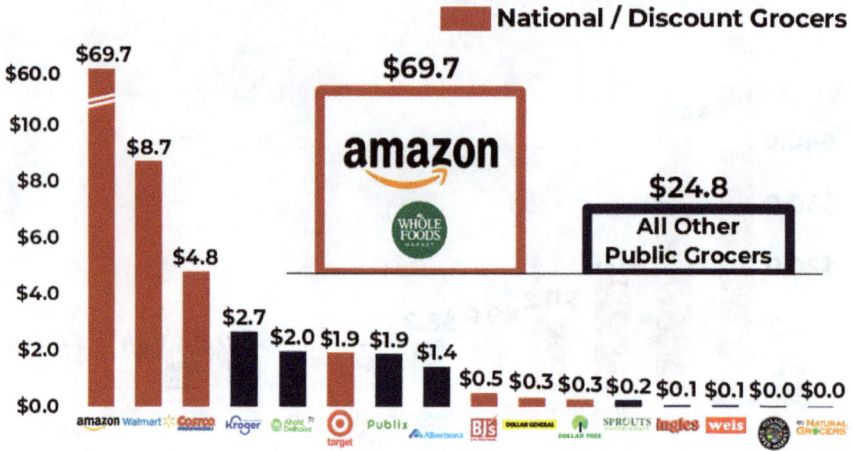

($ in Billions) **EBITDA GROWTH SINCE JANUARY 2020**

Source: Capital IQ as of September 2024.
1) Represents Ahold Delhaize USA segment EBITDA.

Putting this into broader context, supermarket grocers have EBITDA margins that are not only well less than the national/discount grocers, but also well less than the food manufacturers from whom they buy groceries. The aggregate EBITDA margin of a group of prominent food manufacturers is literally four times larger than Kroger, which is well less than Amazon, Dollar General and Walmart.

CPG COMPANIES AND NATIONAL / DISCOUNT GROCERS HAVE SIGNIFICANTLY HIGHER EBITDA MARGINS THAN SUPERMARKET GROCERS

CPG V. GROCER EBITDA MARGINS

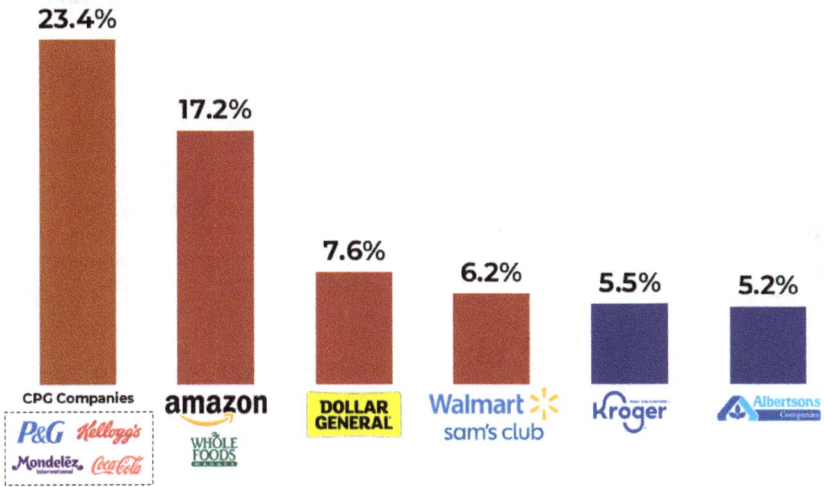

Source: Capital IQ and Company filings as of September 2024. Reflects LTM figures.

Perhaps the clearest indication of relative scale among America's grocers is market valuation. It's a tale of two cities: the valuation of the publicly traded national/discount grocers is exponentially larger than the publicly traded supermarket grocers — 21 times as much, or 95 percent of the total. It is very clear where the market — which values companies based on predictions of growth and future performance — thinks grocery growth will be coming from.

AMERICA'S NATIONAL / DISCOUNT GROCERS HAVE MEANINGFULLY LARGER VALUATIONS THAN SUPERMARKET GROCERS

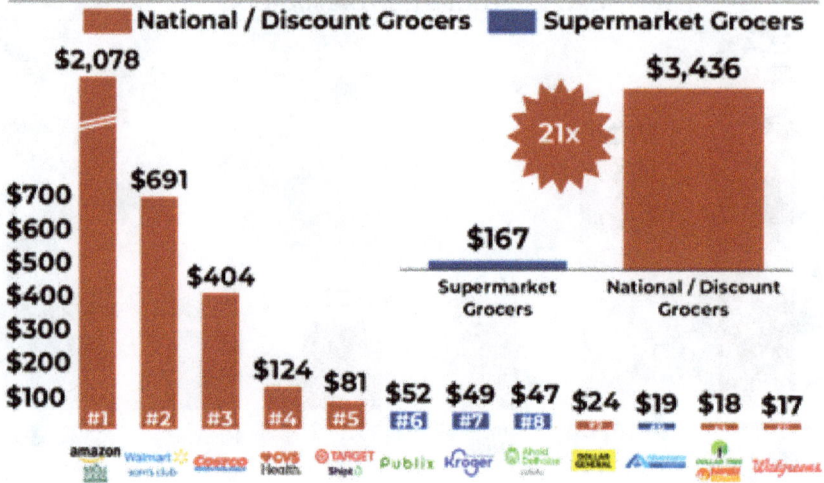

FIRM VALUATION

($ in Billions)

■ National / Discount Grocers   ■ Supermarket Grocers

Source: Capital IQ and Company Filings as of September 2024.

This is even more stark when we look at how much valuation has changed. For perspective, as noted above, Amazon's value is up over **_$1 trillion_** in the past four years and has doubled in value. Costco is up over $270 billion and has tripled in value. Walmart is up over 75 percent, a $300 billion increase. The supermarket grocers are generally up a little bit, but there is simply no comparison.

THE VALUATIONS OF AMERICA'S NATIONAL / DISCOUNT GROCERS HAVE INCREASED FAR MORE DURING THE PANDEMIC THAN SUPERMARKET GROCERS

($ in Billions) **FIRM VALUATION GROWTH SINCE JANUARY 2020**

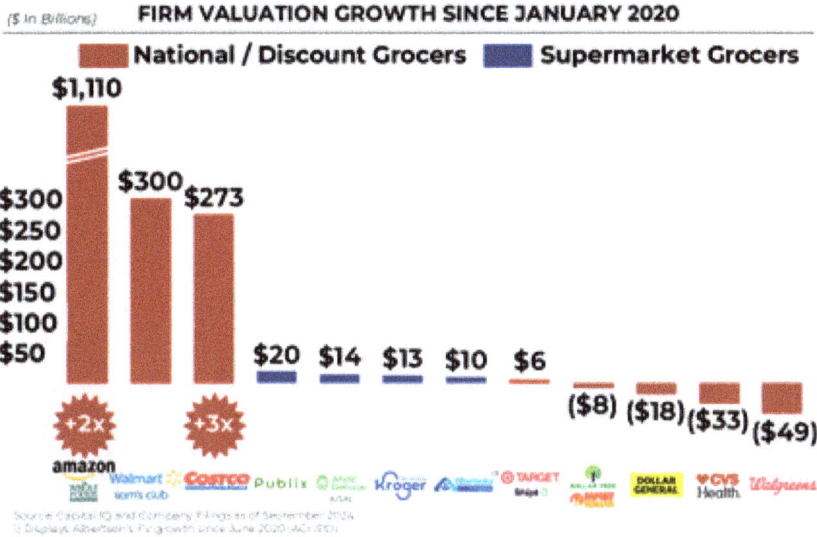

Valuation multiples confirm this: Walmart trades at ~17x EBITDA, Amazon trades at 20x EBITDA, and Costco trades at over 35x EBITDA. Conversely, supermarket grocers like Kroger and Ahold Delhaize trade at 6x EBITDA. It is very clear where investment capital is flowing.

SUPERMARKET GROCERS TRADE AT A STEEP DISCOUNT TO FASTER-GROWING NATIONAL / DISCOUNT GROCERS

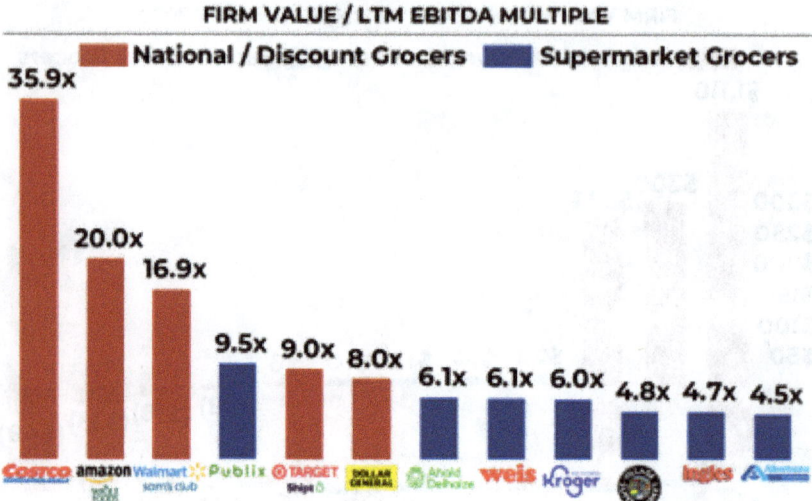

FIRM VALUE / LTM EBITDA MULTIPLE

■ National / Discount Grocers ■ Supermarket Grocers

35.9x — Costco
20.0x — amazon
16.9x — Walmart / Sam's Club
9.5x — Publix
9.0x — TARGET / Shipt
8.0x — DOLLAR GENERAL
6.1x — Ahold Delhaize
6.1x — weis
6.0x — Kroger
4.8x
4.7x — ingles
4.5x — Albertsons

Source: Capital IQ and Company Filings as of September 2024

Speaking of investment, there is a similar dichotomy of capital spending between national/discount grocers and supermarket grocers. As usual, Amazon, Walmart and Costco are, along with Target, at the head of the class; but the degree of collective spending difference is even more astounding. The national/discount grocers spent 90 percent of the total, over 8 times more than their public supermarket grocery peers. These investments in logistics, technology and growth (acquisitions, new stores, etc.) are accelerating the performance distinction between the two groups of grocers.

TOP 15 GROCERS: LAST 5 YEARS CUMULATIVE CAPEX

NATIONAL / DISCOUNT GROCERS LEVERAGE THEIR SCALE TO INVEST BACK IN THEIR BUSINESSES

($ In Billions)

LAST 5-YEARS CUMULATIVE CAPEX

Source: Company filings and publicly available information as of September 2024.

As noted above, grocery is a global business. On a global store count basis among U.S. grocers, the national/discount grocers are particularly dominant. Dollar General and Family Dollar/Dollar Tree together have over 36,000 stores. The two German-owned behemoths Aldi (and its affiliate Trader Joe's) and Lidl together have over 25,000 stores.[49] While drug retailers have been closing unprofitable stores amid similar challenges from Walmart, Costco and Amazon, Walgreens and CVS still have over 20,000 stores. (Rite Aid has just announced the confirmation of a plan to exit bankruptcy with 1,300 stores, roughly 1,000 fewer than when they entered bankruptcy in 2023.) Walmart has over 10,000 stores globally, including Sam's.

Ahold Delhaize, the largest U.S. supermarket grocer by global stores, has fewer than 8,000 stores and is ranked #8. Kroger is only ranked #9.

---

[49] https://info.lidl/en#:~:text=Lidl%20currently%20operates%20around%201 2%2C000,products%20at%20the%20best%20price.

The national/discount grocers on this list have over 99,000 global stores; supermarket grocers have roughly 15,000, less than 15 percent of the total.

MOST U.S. NATIONAL / DISCOUNT GROCERS HAVE THE BENEFIT OF GLOBAL SCALE

GLOBAL STORE COUNT (U.S. GROCERS)[1]

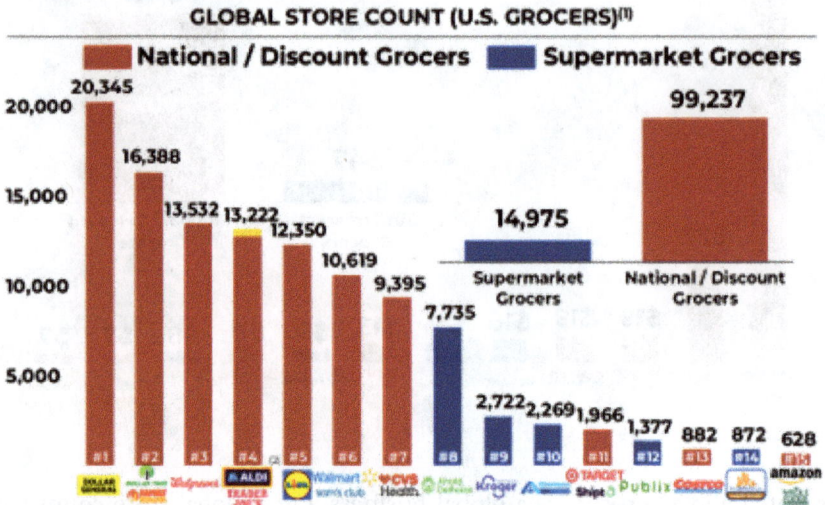

Source: Company Filings & Company Websites as of September 2024.
1) Among grocers with operations in the U.S.
2) Includes Aldi Süd 2023 & Aldi Nord 2022 figures, which represents the latest publicly available information. Pro forma for Winn Dixie and Harveys stores recently acquired.

CHAPTER 4

Grocery Jobs

I put myself through college working as a bartender in Philadelphia. I might have worked part-time at a supermarket had there been any nearby, but there were none at that time. I bought all of my groceries at the nearby CVS, which even then had an ample food offering. That bartending job paid for food, rent and utilities; without it, I don't know how I would have made it through college.

America's grocers are also responsible for millions of rewarding jobs and, by extension, the well-being of millions of families around the country. Some of these jobs are long careers that support families for decades; others are temporary and often part-time, but still highly productive and an important contributor to the great experience so many of our local supermarkets provide us.

Those early part-time jobs that so many of us had, working ourselves through high school and/or college, were often transformative. They not only helped us pay our bills, but they helped us grow into adulthood, appreciate responsibility, build pride in "real world" accomplishments and learn the value of dedicated customer service. These early supermarket jobs helped develop many of the towering figures of our industry, like Jim Donald, Rodney McMullen (CEO of Kroger), Bob Miller (former CEO of Fred Meyer,

Rite Aid and Albertsons), and so many other great leaders at America's grocers and beyond.

As the national/discount grocers have exponentially grown their U.S. grocery businesses, the sales they've built have had to come from somewhere — mostly from supermarket grocers. Consequently, many supermarkets have had to close.

The average supermarket employs about 100 people. When a store needs to close, 100 teammates' jobs (and thus 100 families) are in jeopardy. I've seen it up close; it is gut-wrenching.

While the number of national/discount grocers continues to proliferate at eye-popping levels, there are nearly 1,000 fewer supermarkets today than there were 10 years ago (now totaling less than 26,000). That's roughly 100,000 supermarket jobs lost — **100,000 jobs**. That's 100,000 families, many with children to feed; 100,000 sets of bills; 100,000 American dreams suspended.

Larger supermarket grocers are generally unionized; national/discount grocers are mostly non-union. Across the 25 most populous U.S. markets, while non-union national/discount grocers have increased their store base, unionized grocers have lost stores in most places.

NON-UNION STORE COUNT IN THE MOST POPULOUS U.S. MARKETS IS SURGING

STORE COUNT CHANGES – 2012 TO 2022

As store counts have shifted across the country, market share has shifted as well, with unionized grocers losing share in most of the top American markets. Non-unionized grocers have added share in every one of these markets, in many cases a significant amount.

NON-UNION SHARE IN THE MOST POPULOUS U.S. MARKETS IS SURGING AS WELL (2012-2022)

MARKET SHARE CHANGES – 2012 TO 2022

All of these store and market share changes have had a significant impact on grocery jobs, particularly unionized grocery jobs. Whereas the split between union and non-union jobs was more balanced 20 years ago, unionized grocers' share of jobs among the top 15 grocers has fallen from nearly 40 percent to 14 percent.

NON-UNION GROCERS HAVE TAKEN THE VAST MAJORITY OF AMERICAN GROCERY JOBS IN THE PAST 20 YEARS

UNION VS. NON-UNION JOB SHARE – TOP 15 GROCERS

2003	2023
Union 39% / Non-Union 61%	Union 14% / Non-Union 86%

Non-Union Grocers +25%

Unionized Grocers -25%

Note: Represents Top 15 U.S. Grocers in 2003 and 2023.

There have been way too many supermarket jobs lost, way too many communities robbed of a supermarket pillar and pivotal early job experience for their future leaders. It's unlikely that a replacement job at an Amazon fulfillment center (while they last, before they are automated away) offers the same rewarding experience of engagement with our neighbors.

The bar I worked at during college closed during the pandemic. If I were in college now and that happened, I would not have been able to get to the outskirts of town to work at the Walmart or the Amazon fulfillment center to which many jobs are effectively migrating. I wouldn't have been able to afford to get there; I'm not sure how I would have been able to pay my bills and remain sufficiently focused on school. My story likely would have been different. I doubt I'd be writing this today.

But America's supermarket grocers still employ well over two million people, with over two million families relying on them, and on us.

SUPERMARKET GROCERS EMPLOY 2.4 MILLION AMERICANS

Supermarket Stores and Employees		
Grocers	**Grocery Stores**	**Employees**
Kroger	2,722	407,000
Albertsons	2,269	285,000
Publix	1,377	253,000
Ahold Delhaize	2,048	229,000
H-E-B	435	160,000
HyVee	285	93,000
Wakefern	365	80,000
Wegmans	110	53,000
giant eagle	216	36,000
SPROUTS	419	32,000
UNFI	75	29,455
ingles	198	26,420
MARKET BASKET	88	25,000
weis	196	23,000
WinCo FOODS	140	20,000
C&S Wholesale Grocers	165	15,000
Other U.S. Grocers	~14,700	~600,000
Total	**~25,800**	**~2,400,000**

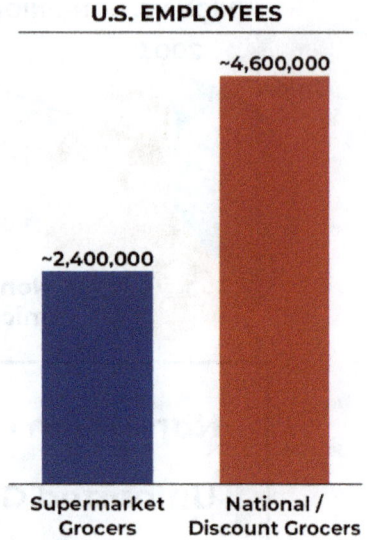

Source: Company filings and publicly available information.

U.S. EMPLOYEES

~4,600,000

~2,400,000

Supermarket Grocers

National / Discount Grocers

CHAPTER 5

Rays of Light in the Storm

There's a wonderful world where all you desire
And everything you've longed for is at your fingertips
Where the bittersweet taste of life is at your lips
Where aisles and aisles of dreams await you
The cool promise of ecstasy fills the air
At the end of each working day she's waiting there...

– Bruce Springsteen — *Queen of the Supermarket*

Grocery headwinds are most certainly daunting, but there remain some extraordinary supermarket grocers across the country doing extraordinary things to overcome the odds and maintain a strong position in their local markets. Many of these grocers are family businesses run by third- or fourth-generation owners.

While consumers regularly shop at more than five different grocers, when they ultimately decide where (or how) to make a given trip (or online order) for groceries, they are choosing between price, convenience and experience.

Price and Convenience vs. Connection and Trust

There is no denying that the world is increasingly transactional, largely dictated by price and convenience. Few supermarket grocers are ever going to be able to match Walmart, Costco, Aldi or Dollar General on price, and that is only getting harder as those market leaders continue to grow their grocery businesses, generate efficiencies, and invest even more in price, wages, marketing and technology to acquire and retain customers.

In convenience, mainly in online grocery delivery, Amazon remains the clear leader; but Walmart has made significant investments in its version of Prime, Walmart+, with which it is making great strides, particularly with the savings this subscription offers its members. Target remains formidable as well, with Shipt and Deliv meaningfully improving their online convenience value proposition.

However, while online grocery continues to gain momentum across the country, particularly in more densely populated markets where delivery economics are more manageable, leading local grocery leaders remember that stores still account for roughly 90 percent of U.S. grocery sales. Even if online grocery were to double in the next five-plus years, as predicted by some industry analysts, it will still be only 20 percent of sales. ***Stores will still make up 80 percent of the industry*** and an even larger share of the profit.

Leading local grocers recognize that their customer relationships are their most valuable asset. There are too many examples around the country to mention them all here, but the core of their common success is constant reinforcement of their deep relationship of trust with customers. This trust was built, in many cases, on decades of connection that for many people — consciously or subconsciously — hearkens back to the kind of gleeful grocery experience that Dickens describes in *A Christmas Carol*, which inspired this book.

Supermarket Differentiation Techniques

The ethos of this warm approach evokes the lessons learned watching Jim Donald walk the aisles of Pathmark's stores. Jim would encourage his teammates — whom he called "the front lines" — to engage with customers like family, constantly improving the company's connection with customers. He would solicit direct feedback from store teammates to learn about deficiencies or other suggestions to help the company improve. After all, nobody knows customers better than the folks serving them every day. This incidentally had another benefit. At both Pathmark and Haggen, when Jim joined the companies to became CEO, shrink was a real problem. By more directly engaging with teammates and instituting a program among teammates to identify and report theft, cashier "sweet-hearting" and other shrink, he helped both companies generate significant savings that had a significant impact on the P&L.

The dynamics in every market are a little different, but there are some common themes in how our best regional grocers across the country work to protect customer relationships and win back lost trips. Some grocers are hyper-focused on local products, from regional farmers to nearby manufacturers; this appeals to many customers who take pride in supporting their hometown. Other grocers are focused on pinnacle premium quality products to drive differentiation and justify higher prices. Health, sourcing and sustainability increasingly drive customer purchase decisions; making that information available drives trust and connection. Prepared food and seating convert some stores into quasi-restaurants, becoming a "grocerant" destination — and limiting shrink (many people — perhaps including you — deride the term "grocerant"; but it drives loyalty and profit, so call it whatever you'd like). Some grocers are highly connected to the community through philanthropy, supporting local organizations like little leagues and other youth organizations. Store events that are fun for customers of all ages can be highly differentiated and hard to disrupt. In-store animatronic characters — like at my local store, Stew Leonard's — transform a grocery trip to a Disney-like grocery adventure that kids (and parents) want to do again and again. (On a personal note, Stew Leonard's is hands-down the most fun I've had in a grocery store; its CEO Stew Leonard Jr. is also one of the warmest, most engaging and family-oriented leaders I've met in my career.)

While Kroger and Albertsons are in various regions of the country (though not yet national), they are both ultimately federations of local grocers. They have been making investments to build ecosystems that have both great stores and differentiated omnichannel experiences. Online pickup ("click & collect") or buy online/pickup in store (a.k.a. "BOPIS") options have become a core part of their offering, enhancing convenience while still bringing customers in the store. As Jim Donald (who was recently CEO of Albertsons and remains Chairman), likes to say, they've gone from "four walls to no walls."

The Rise of Ethnic and Premium/Health Specialty Grocery

Another great example of successful differentiation is the many specialty and ethnic grocers around the country which have created an authenticity moat that has proven to be decisive as they continue to grow and take grocery share in numerous markets. Latino grocers use tortillerías, distinctive meat cuts, and prepared food and drinks, along with creative music, fun events and store decorations that evoke former home countries of customers, many of whom are first- or second-generation immigrants. Asian grocers offer fresh quality, highly differentiated merchandise and live seafood to deliver an experience that is simply not replicable by any national/discount grocers.

What many people don't appreciate is just how pervasive specialty grocers have become. There are over 2,700 specialty grocery stores in the United States, including over 1,600 ethnic grocers (about 1,200 Latino stores and roughly 400 Asian-focused stores) and over 1,100 premium/health-oriented specialty grocers. All of these stores offer a distinctive experience, in many cases becoming a destination that is very difficult for national/discount grocers to replicate, particularly when those national/discount grocers just include a perfunctory set of SKUs in their attempt to cater to the given group.

THERE ARE OVER 2,700 ETHNIC AND PREMIUM/HEALTH SPECIALTY GROCERY STORES IN THE U.S. (AND GROWING)

Format	# of Stores
Asian	408
Latino	1,214
Premium/ Health	1,103
Total	2,725

Source: Company websites and publicly available information.

The specialty grocers are expected to continue to grow in significant numbers in the next few years. Their customers tend to be far more loyal and their financials are generally superior to traditional supermarket grocers. These stores, many of which are owned by wonderful immigrant families, are great examples of courageous grocery change-makers at work. Change can be difficult to implement, but many of these specialty operators have found a way to rise above the challenges and create something truly extraordinary.

Confronting Change-Maker Challenges

There are many good examples of organizations that have meaningfully evolved over the past few years. Kroger with dunnhumby and Ocado; Price

Chopper with its exceptional Market 32 transformation; C&S building a transformational retail footprint to complement its supply heritage; Sprouts Farmers Market accelerating growth with a more-efficient store footprint; the list goes on and on. That said, many organizations have not evolved. They often get mired in what I call "change-maker challenges."

Being a change-maker takes not only courage, but also a lot of hard work. Let's use technological evolution as an example. Practically speaking, to make a significant technological change that will likely impact the entire company, somebody on your team, if not a series of people, will need to: invest time to research evolution partners; go to tech conferences or generally invest significant time to meet and screen candidates and then choose the best candidate; present internally to committee; endure the sharp elbows of resistance; and continue to push the change through to roll out a test. When there are inevitable bumps, they'll need to weather the doubters and keep pushing through to achieve a successful implementation.

I've worked with countless executives. Not everyone has the constitution required to drive change. But the best executives — the best leaders — are strategic in charting a course, decisive in pursuing it, nimble in evolving through challenges, and are constantly exhibiting irrepressible grit and the guts to stick with it once it's live.

People want to be led well. Great team leaders make for great teams. Grocery executives have the power to make a huge difference in people's lives, for their teams, their customers and their communities.

I often remind folks to be willing to fail, learn and iterate, just like Amazon, because Amazon's not messing around — and they have your customers' data. Coming back to our technology example, keep this in mind: *grocers need to become tech companies before tech companies become grocers.*

While the formula varies, it all comes down to experience and trust. Evolving is not easy, but it is necessary. Don't be sheep — be shepherds. As Abraham Lincoln (and then Jamie Dimon) said, *"Good things may come to those who wait, but only those things left by those who hustle."*

In short, give people more of a reason to want their family to be part of your family. And while grit is necessary to evolve and compete with the national/discount grocers, it's much, much easier to afford to make these changes when you're larger and have more capacity to pay for them. That's where mergers and acquisitions come into focus.

CHAPTER 6

Grocery Mergers & Acquisitions

Although the grocery industry has experienced a great deal of consolidation over the past several decades, it remains the largest and most fragmented retail sector. In the U.K. and Canada, the top five grocers have 74 percent and 79 percent market share, respectively; in the United States, it is roughly 60 percent, and that's only because Walmart has 30 percent share (and growing).

AMERICAN GROCERY REMAINS FAR LESS CONCENTRATED THAN GLOBAL PEERS

THE TOP 5 GROCERS IN CANADA AND THE UK HAVE 79% AND 74% MARKET SHARE, RESPECTIVELY, IN THE UNITED STATES IT IS ROUGHLY 60%

% GROCERY SHARE FOR THE TOP 5 GROCERS BY COUNTRY

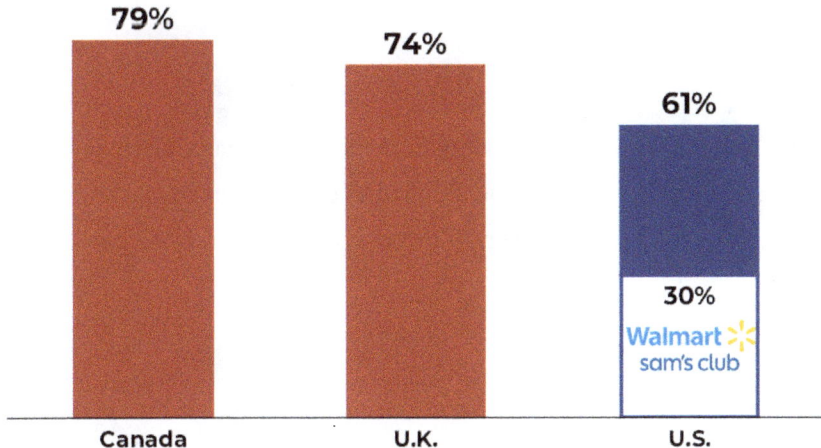

79%		
	74%	
		61%
		30%
		Walmart sam's club
Canada	**U.K.**	**U.S.**

Source: UK data represents just Great Britain and is from Kantar World Panel as of September 2024. Canadian Data from Government of Canada, December 2023 report. U.S. Data per Solomon estimates using company filings and Capital IQ.

Some supermarket grocers, like HEB and Publix, are clear market leaders with exceptional density across large swaths of two enormous states, Texas and Florida, respectively.

HEB, America's #9 grocer, has extraordinary market share in Texas. Notwithstanding relentless competition from Walmart, HEB has over 40 percent share in over 60 percent of its markets and over 30 percent share in 80 percent of its markets.

HEB, AMERICA'S #9 GROCER, MAINTAINS OVER 40% SHARE IN 63% OF ITS MARKETS

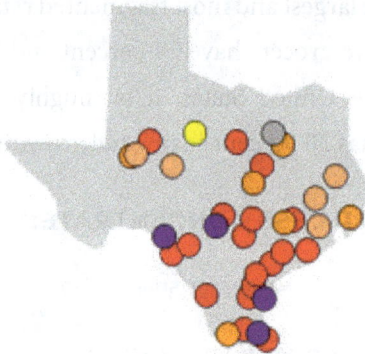

H·E·B

Market Share
- >50% (4 markets, 11% of markets)
- >40% (22 markets, 63% of markets)
- >30% (28 markets, 80% of markets)
- >20% (33 markets, 94% of markets)
- >10% (34 markets, 97% of markets)
- >0% (35 markets, 100% of markets)

Source: Chain Store Guide (CSG) Grocery Market Share Studies.
Note: Market share data consists of data from core-based statistical area across the US. Does not include online grocery fulfilled outside of stores.

Publix, America's #8 grocer, is similar. While Publix has a broader footprint beyond its home state, in Florida, Publix has over 40 percent share in over 30 percent of its markets and over 30 percent share in nearly 70 percent of its markets.

PUBLIX, AMERICA'S #8 GROCER, MAINTAINS OVER 40% SHARE IN 31% OF ITS FLORIDA MARKETS

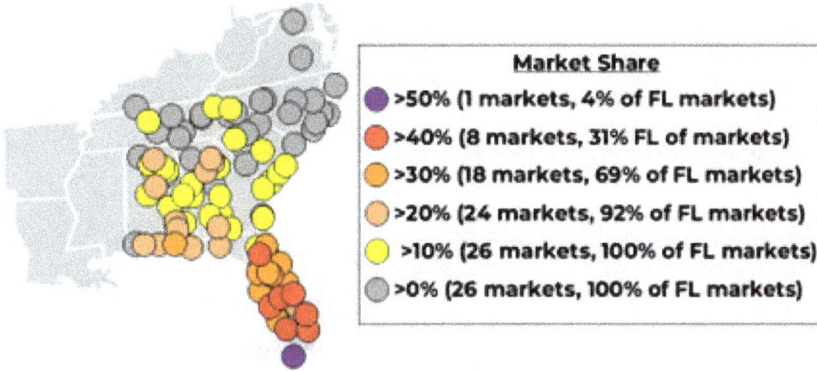

Publix

Market Share

● >50% (1 markets, 4% of FL markets)
● >40% (8 markets, 31% FL of markets)
● >30% (18 markets, 69% of FL markets)
○ >20% (24 markets, 92% of FL markets)
○ >10% (26 markets, 100% of FL markets)
○ >0% (26 markets, 100% of FL markets)

Source: Chain Store Guide (CSG) Grocery Market Share Studies.
Note: Market share data consists of data from cone-based statistical area across the US. Does not include online grocery fulfilled outside of stores. Data in map legend reflects just Florida market share.

Most supermarket grocers don't have anything remotely resembling this amount of local market share. By comparison, while Walmart has over 40 percent share in 55 percent of its markets, Kroger and Albertsons combined would have over 40 percent share in just 8 percent of their markets, and this is before the pending divestitures to C&S, which would reduce that figure significantly.

WALMART, HEB AND PUBLIX LEAD MOST OF THEIR MARKETS; KROGER/ALBERTSONS SHARE IS MODEST BY COMPARISON

% OF MARKETS WITH >40% SHARE

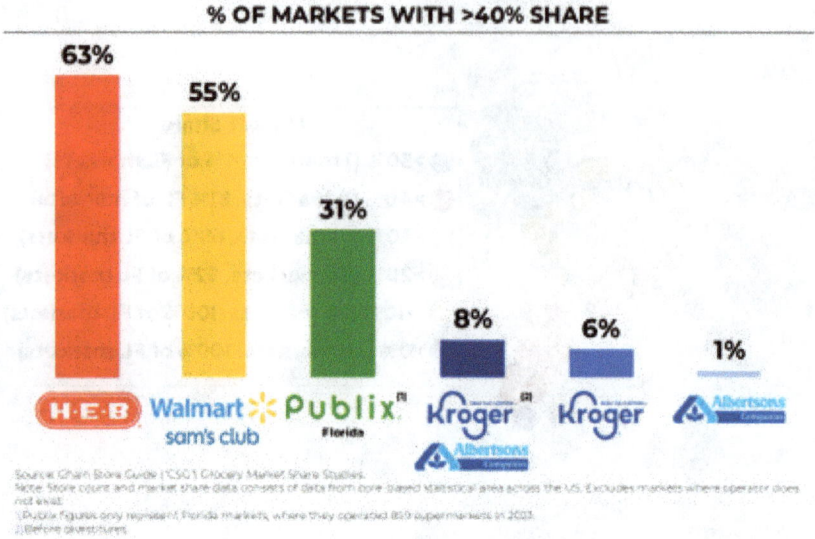

Source: Chain Store Guide (CSG) Grocery Market Share Studies.
Note: Store count and market share data consists of data from core-based statistical area across the US. Excludes markets where operator does not exist.
1) Publix figures only represent Florida markets, where they operated 850 supermarkets in 2023.
2) Before divestitures.

For companies with the capacity to open new stores, the inflationary dynamics of the past few years have made organic store growth prohibitively expensive in many cases. The price of construction teams, building material, store fixtures and equipment have all shifted the build-versus-buy calculus meaningfully toward the latter option.

This is why grocery mergers and acquisitions are so important for supermarket grocers, particularly in light of the sector's transformation and continued share loss to the national/discount grocers. If Walmart, Costco and Amazon are driving lower price and convenience advantages, supermarket grocers need to find ways to afford the operational initiatives and investments required to better compete and strengthen their relationships of trust with customers.

M&A Cost Savings (Synergies)

Grocery M&A transactions that are well-planned and integrated usually create considerable cost savings — synergies — that yield financial benefits to buyers or owners of the merged companies. Here are a few examples, which are easily summarized as you move down the P&L.

Cost-of-Goods Synergies

National Brands and Fresh — Improve costs from vendors with higher volume; harmonize variance by SKU (negotiating with vendors to get the lower of the prices charged to each company across individual products), rationalize less-productive items

Private Label — Improve costs of product with higher volume; rationalize packaging cost; optimize formulations

Distribution — Enhance warehouse productivity; statistically optimize truck routes over larger number of stores to reduce miles, energy and labor cost; better bracket pricing with more volume

Store Synergies

Personnel Expenses — Enhance labor scheduling efficiency, harmonize training and performance-incentive best practices to drive better in-store service (which should improve store performance)

Store Expenses — RFPs on supplies, safety and sanitation costs

Goods Not for Resale — Optimize costs of packaging, carriages, bags, in-store utensils and other supplies

Corporate Synergies

Corporate Personnel — Back-office function efficiencies, e.g., IT, HR, legal and finance

Corporate Functions — Use scale to create efficiencies in marketing and advertising (circular production, digital marketing, social media) and professional service providers

Corporate Contracts — Renegotiate key contracts (insurance, communications, benefits, banking, armored cars), streamline IT (hardware and software maintenance, software licenses and data center costs); implement best-in-class corporate policies; credit card processing fees

<u>Financing Synergies</u>

Cost of Debt — Larger sales base should lead to better credit rating, which lowers borrowing costs

Lower Rent — Renegotiate leases to reflect higher credit quality, improved ratings (better cap rate on leases)

These savings can be very significant. In some transactions we have executed, the cost savings have been larger than the pre-transaction EBITDA of either merging company. The additional cash flow from these savings can be used to support lower prices, better wages, more marketing, enhanced logistics, stronger technology and accelerated growth initiatives. There's also a great deal of value to be captured for company shareholders as owners of a bigger, stronger company.

Undermining Customer Trust vs. Back-End Savings

Many grocery mergers in the 1990s were viewed to have been unsuccessful, as various businesses were stripped of their local differentiation in ways customers noticed immediately, thereby disturbing their connection with the grocer and diminishing trust. However, in the years that followed, strategic acquirers have been extremely careful to learn from — and not repeat — the mistakes of transactions past. They have focused their cost-saving efforts on the back-end areas noted above. When done right, shoppers should not notice much of a difference, except the roll-out of store-level services, technology and other best-practice improvements to customer experience.

As a result, the vast majority of strategic transactions in the past decade have been very successful, and many of America's largest grocers have grown by acquisition. Walmart, Amazon, Target and Costco have all made significant acquisitions, some in grocery and some to better develop their ecosystems and enhance their ability to serve customers. Kroger, Albertsons, Ahold Delhaize Giant Eagle, Sprouts, Good Food Holdings and Heritage Grocers are all the products of various mergers and acquisitions.

MANY OF AMERICA'S LARGEST GROCERS HAVE GROWN BY STRATEGIC CONSOLIDATION

Source: Capital IQ, Crunch Base, Pitchbook.
1) Costco and CCM entered a joint venture in 1992 to establish a Costco branch in Mexico. Costco acquired the entire branch in 2012.

Hotel Consolidation Parallel

Grocery consolidation in search of efficiencies across numerous formats is fairly similar to what has happened in the hotel industry over the past two decades. Each of the major hotel companies, including Marriott, Hilton, Hyatt and InterContinental, has executed several acquisitions, involving over 11,000 hotels, in an effort to capture similar efficiencies.

HOTEL CHAIN ACQUISITIONS

Overcoming Resistance to Grocery Mergers

Some grocery owners are highly resistant to sales or mergers, for various reasons. I am very sensitive to and deeply respect the focus on independence, particularly in an effort to protect family legacy where a company has been a pillar of its community for generations. However, I am reminded of some sage advice I once heard from the owner of a venture capital firm:

"There's dilution and there's death; dilution's better."

One might suggest that I'm biased on the benefits of scale because I'm in the mergers business; *but that fact doesn't make all of these other facts any less true*. This is <u>not</u> "fake news" — <u>it's real grocery math</u>.

Building scale with mergers and acquisitions is indisputably one of the best means by which regional grocers can enable their stores to continue to be competitive, continue to serve their communities and — for family grocers — maintain their legacy. Far too many grocers have either been either unwilling to take a clear-eyed look at the reality of their declining performance or unwilling to sufficiently understand the rising tide of industry changes, in an ocean of powerful competitors, until things have gotten out of control. They often contact us two years too late, when their options are no longer good, and they have little real choice but to proceed toward a distressed sale.

The best-positioned (and best-led) companies regularly engage in transparent dialogue about benchmarked performance changes, operating risks, competitive challenges and strategic alternatives to alleviate these challenges. These topics are a consistent component of every quarterly or monthly board conversation.

I often say that we have two covenants with our clients: first, to keep their secrets, because confidentiality is inviolable; second, to preserve value, which requires a constant, eyes-open review of this calculus.

With that said, even the most sensible and necessary business developments can get into the crosshairs of a politically-motivated regulatory regime. That brings us to the FTC.

CHAPTER 7

FTC

The Federal Trade Commission has been charged with protecting Americans for over 100 years. The mandate of the FTC — to protect consumers from anti-competitive companies — is critically important, particularly during challenging inflationary periods.

When supermarket grocers merge, the combined company's stores will almost always still compete with a long list of grocers, including supercenters, club grocers, drugstores, dollar and discount grocers, specialty/ethnic grocers and online grocers.

However, when evaluating grocery mergers, the FTC has been defining the "grocery market" *for decades* in the same narrow, anachronistic and, frankly, indefensible manner — as traditional supermarkets. This is plainly inconsistent with the realities of the present-day grocery marketplace and rests on assumptions that are demonstrably false to any grocery shopper, and certainly to anyone in the industry.

The FTC's posture directly undermines the increasingly existential scale-building efforts by regional supermarket grocers as their viability is challenged by the much larger, far better capitalized national/discount grocers like Walmart, Target, Costco, Amazon/Whole Foods, Aldi, Trader Joe's and Dollar General.

Paradoxically, this calculus benefits the very national/discount grocers that the FTC has professed the need to rein in, thereby enabling them as they get bigger and stronger, taking more customers and making it harder for smaller supermarket grocers to survive in the long run.

When the FTC forces supermarket grocers to waste many months (if not years) proving the extremely competitive nature of their markets — a fact that is obvious to any reasonable observer (and any grocery shopper) — it is effectively putting its thumb on the scale to help the national/discount grocers preserve and expand their dominance. That may not be the FTC's intention, but it undeniably is the result. It's not fair, and it's not good for the country.

EVERY DAY THE FTC DELAYS SUPERMARKET GROCERS FROM BUILDING THEIR CAPACITY TO COMPETE HELPS SUPPORT THE VAST AND GROWING POWER OF NATIONAL / DISCOUNT GROCERS

A "Grocery Market" Definition from the 1980s

The FTC has historically argued — including in its crusade against Kroger/Albertsons — that national/discount grocers are not part of the relevant grocery "market" because they do not have a supermarket's full complement of products and services. They are not viewed by FTC orthodoxy to be "adequate substitutes for supermarkets," even though most Americans regularly shop at numerous such "substitutes." Many national/discount grocers are therefore excluded from the FTC's view of the "grocery market" when evaluating grocery mergers, as are online grocers, whose rapidly growing sales are also essentially excluded.

To demonstrate how ridiculous this is, think of all the places your family has shopped for groceries in the past few weeks. Let's take one example: Niraj Komatineni from my team is from Cincinnati, Kroger's hometown. He recently asked his parents where they shop for groceries and reported their answer:

> *"They got their eggs, milk, meat, condiments, some fruit and vegetables from Costco. They got household items, cereals, beauty and personal care items and school/office supplies from Walmart. They got select produce, protein bars, ice cream, frozen food, medicine and snacks from Kroger. They got organic produce and meat from Whole Foods. They got Indian produce, vegetables, snacks from Patel Brothers. Finally, anything they couldn't easily get from those stores, or forgot, they got delivered from Amazon. This is all in the suburbs of Cincinnati where we have all of those stores – two Costcos, three Krogers, Walmart, Whole Foods, Patel Brothers, Meijer, Aldi, Sam's, Fresh Thyme, Fresh Market and two Targets – all within 10 or 15 minutes of our house. The local grocery market contains all of these operators, so it only makes sense to consider them all competitors because each purchase at one takes dollars away from the others. They all have their own unique*

SKUs, so you almost need to go to all of them to get all the groceries you want."

That's eleven different grocers, in Kroger's hometown, plus Amazon online.

As noted earlier, Walmart, Target, Costco and Amazon are also America's leading online grocers; they all offer delivery services that meaningfully widen the radius of customers whose grocery business they are able to compete for, in many cases without having a store nearby. With Instacart, customers have never been more easily able to conveniently price-check across numerous grocers on their smartphone, building a basket that can be picked up or delivered whenever they want, at will, in most U.S. markets, whether on the Instacart marketplace or online with any of Walmart, Target, Costco or Amazon. (In other words, without having to drive to multiple grocers to check prices, as we all needed to do until just a few years ago.) As noted above, online grocery has quadrupled in the past four years and is expected to continue to grow at a rapid pace in the next few years.

While the FTC rightfully aims to ensure that grocers do not employ monopolistic pricing power, in 2024 (as opposed to 1984, when its market definition was more fairly employed), there has never been more pricing transparency quite literally at our fingertips. As such, it is nearly impossible for a smaller supermarket grocer to meaningfully raise prices without losing countless customers to the lower-priced, ubiquitous national/discount grocers.

FTC Chair Acknowledges National/Discount Grocers

Ironically, FTC Chair Lina Khan herself predicted these competitive challenges for supermarket grocers in a June 2017 *New York Times* op-ed,[50] which was published in the wake of Amazon's Whole Foods acquisition

---

[50] https://www.nytimes.com/2017/06/21/opinion/amazon-whole-foods-jeff-bezos.html

(when its market valuation was *"only"* **~$460 billion**). Given that you can't be a rival of something you're not, Khan clearly conceded Amazon is a grocer:

CHAIR LINA KHAN PRESCIENTLY PREDICTED AMAZON'S RAPID GROCERY GROWTH AND CONSEQUENCES ON RIVAL GROCERS

The New York Times

Amazon Bites Off Even More Monopoly Power

By Lina M. Khan
June 21, 2017

"Buying Whole Foods will enable Amazon to leverage and amplify the extraordinary power it enjoys in online markets and delivery, making an even greater share of commerce part of its fief...*By bundling services and integrating grocery stores into its logistics network, <u>the company will be able to shut out or disfavor rival grocers</u>.*"

Source:

The prior sections of this book confirm Khan's prescience. The analyses demonstrate the waning relative strength and receding ability of supermarket grocers to endure the ongoing share usurpation by the national/discount grocers (particularly Walmart, Costco and Amazon), whose scale brings a stronger credit rating that yields the very low cost of capital required to make investments not only in customer acquisition and retention, but in employee wages and ongoing employment.

The FTC's own staff report on the American food chain in 2024 acknowledges that Walmart and Amazon are major grocery retailers.[51] The USDA, which is apparently far closer than the FTC to the facts on how people feed their

---

[51] https://www.ftc.gov/reports/feeding-america-time-crisis-ftc-staff-report-united-states-grocery-supply-chain-covid-19-pandemic

families, allows individuals to use SNAP dollars (food stamps) to buy groceries at supercenters, club, discount, dollar, drug, specialty/ethnic and online grocers, and these grocers account for roughly 50 percent of SNAP dollars spent. One might think the FTC would follow their lead.[52]

Important Points from FTC Listening Forum

In June 2022, before the Kroger/Albertsons merger was announced, the FTC held a Merger Guidelines Listening Forum video conference to hear from members of the public about the effects of mergers and acquisitions on a range of market participants. FTC Chair Lina Khan and then-FTC Commissioners Noah Phillips, Rebecca Slaughter, Christine Wilson and Alvaro Bedoya all attended the event, which included brief remarks from distinguished speakers representing a wide range of industries. There were a variety of astute, objectively incontrovertible points made that one might have hoped at the time would help advance the FTC's "grocery market" definition to reflect modern market dynamics.

Commissioner Phillips, a Republican appointee who resigned not long after this panel, provided particularly insightful perspective on the state of the grocery industry, consumer challenges and the importance of mergers in enabling grocers to become large enough to be able to afford to keep prices lower for customers and mitigate the impact of the significant inflation being experienced across the country:

> *Our nation is emerging from one crisis, the Covid-19 pandemic, and is well into another. As we face historic inflation, Americans are struggling to fill up their gas tanks and feed their families. We want to encourage companies big and small to enter and grow to meet consumer demand during this time. We want them to be more efficient so that they*

---

[52] https://www.numerator.com/snap-shopper-scorecard/

can drive down costs and pass the savings on to consumers. Competition-enhancing mergers and acquisitions is one way they do that. M&A benefits consumers by spurring innovation, improving quality and lowering prices. Smaller firms can join forces to compete more effectively and efficiently against larger rivals; combining can put financially struggling firms on firmer footing and lower their cost of [the] capital...they need to spend in order to grow. Traditional retailers, for example, have seen reduced investment and bankruptcy as they face competition from the Amazons and Walmarts of the world. Combining — merging — can help them compete...[D]iscouraging efficiency, and failing to put consumers first, will mean higher prices.[53]

One speaker in the forum was Mark Gross, a 25-year grocery industry veteran, who is Co-Chairman of Northeast Grocery Inc. (the product of the merger between Price Chopper/Market 32 and Tops Friendly Markets). At the time of the forum, Mark was Executive Chairman of Southeastern Grocers (which then comprised Winn-Dixie, Harveys Supermarket and Fresco y Mas, before its sale to Aldi in early 2024) and a director at Acosta. He also is the former CEO of the hybrid grocery wholesale/retailer Supervalu (now part of United Natural Foods Inc.) and former co-president of hybrid grocery wholesale/retailer C&S Wholesale Grocers.

Gross began his testimony by articulating three key clear conclusions:

1. *"We have to fully update our definition of the grocery market to include all non-traditional grocers, whether they offer what we perceive as a full shop or not."*

---

[53] https://www.ftc.gov/system/files/ftc_gov/pdf/FTC-Merger-Guidelines-Listening-Forum%2C-June-21-2022.pdf

2. *"We need to understand the economic dominance of these non-traditional grocers and how they assert that power."*

3. *"To foster competition [with the national/discount grocers], we need to be more accommodating of regional grocers' merger activity."*

Gross explained that the growth of national/discount grocers has resulted in the reduction of traditional supermarket grocery stores. He added that national/discount grocers are the primary store for most consumers, who shop at multiple channels and banners every week, and declared that this fact does not seem properly reflected when the FTC measures the grocery market and market share.

> *"Because of the economic dominance of the grocery market by a handful of companies," Gross argued, "the market has to be viewed in its entirety of who is competing in this space and who yields market power."*

In demonstrating the economic dominance of America's national/discount grocers, Gross observed that Walmart's capex spending in 2021 was $13 billion, more than half of which (over $7 billion) was on technology. A regional grocer, he noted, will spend at most $200 million on capex, of which only about $20 million is on technology. That $20 million spend versus $7 billion is *"disproportionate,"* he said.

Gross also talked about the merger completed in 2021 between Price Chopper/Market 32 and Tops in upstate New York (on which, in full disclosure, I advised Price Chopper). For background, operating pressures Tops experienced from national/discount grocers such as Amazon, Walmart, Aldi, Dollar General and Family Dollar were instrumental in forcing it into bankruptcy in 2018. Tops was fortunately able to avoid liquidation and emerge from bankruptcy in 2019; but it remained too small to sufficiently compete on its own with the fast-growing national/discount grocers:

"The transaction was pro-competitive, enabling stores to offer better choice for consumers vis-à-vis the giants and enabling the merged company to generate various improvements and leverage technology spend, which helps us to operate more effectively and better serve our customers and our 30,000 associates ... in over 100 communities."

Finally, in arguing that the FTC should properly recognize the market dominance of the grocery giants and their ubiquity as leading online grocers, Gross lamented:

"Our team spent nine months explaining this to the [FTC] staff and compliance officers. ... We spent countless hours and millions of dollars demonstrating that Aldi and Dollar General are bona-fide grocers who sell the same merchandise we do. ... Amazon, Walmart and Target are the largest American online grocers, and they sell a lot of food in our markets."

Another speaker at the conference, Stephanie Martz, the Chief Administrative Officer and General Counsel of the National Retail Federation, made an important point regarding the calculus that the FTC uses in evaluating the competitive market for potential mergers. She argued that the FTC must also incorporate e-commerce competitors in addition to brick-and-mortar players:

"I can't emphasize this enough: it seems inconsistent to express concern, on the one hand, that some of these e-commerce players are too large, and on the other, fail to account for their effect on individual market segments."

Some have argued to the FTC that consolidation among supermarket grocers should be limited and that the only path to more effective competition in the market is to more aggressively enforce the Robinson-Patman Act, which would, they suggest, equalize the wholesale price of grocery staples. Their argument is that if a small grocer pays the same price for milk as Walmart, competition problems will take care of themselves.

While there are various flaws in this argument, I would focus on one in particular: Robinson-Patman would not level the playing field as its proponents suggest. While national/discount grocers do use their scale to negotiate lower costs from suppliers (that they then pass on to consumers, which is why grocery costs as a percentage of household income have come down so much over the years), equalizing the cost of those products would not alleviate the extreme scale difference they enjoy. The inherent benefits of that scale — including a lower cost of capital, more efficient distribution and logistics, cheaper store and corporate contracts, and higher profitability from basic fixed-cost leverage — gives these national/discount grocers an extraordinary advantage that would not be undone by effectively raising the price of milk and eggs at Walmart, Target and Costco. To the contrary, this would just exacerbate the inflationary challenges consumers have been experiencing.

Robinson-Patman is effectively corporate socialism that stifles innovation and disincentivizes the efficiencies that help keep grocery prices lower for consumers.

However, when supermarket grocers are allowed to merge and gain the benefits of incremental scale to create cost savings, consumers benefit because there are better options available to them to shop at stronger, more efficient grocers that can offer lower prices on more goods. Larger, more consolidated supermarket grocers, while still much smaller than the national/discount grocers, might finally be able to exert some restraint on these global behemoths, which have not faced serious competition for many years and continue to grow at a staggering rate.

Kroger/Albertsons[54]

In October 2022, Kroger and Albertsons announced they would be merging in a transaction whereby Kroger would effectively be acquiring Albertsons for $24.6 billion in cash. At the time, Kroger had over 2,700 stores and Albertsons had nearly 2,300. It would be the largest merger of supermarket grocers in American history.

The announcement came just 25 days before Election Day, making the transaction an easy target for politicians across the country, particularly as food inflation had begun to soar in the wake of Russia's invasion of Ukraine in February of that year.

There was widespread reaction — including congressional hearings — in which various politicians both at the national and state levels decried the merger with a series of claims that were demonstrably false. It was as if they were all provided the same talking points that were rife with exaggeration and inaccuracy. The FTC made the same arguments when it ultimately filed its complaint in February 2024 seeking to block the transaction. The attorneys general of Arizona, California, D.C., Illinois, Maryland, Nevada, New Mexico, Oregon and Wyoming all joined the FTC's case; Washington and Colorado filed separate state lawsuits.

The FTC's Disingenuous Claims

- The FTC claimed that supermarket grocers like Kroger and Albertsons were responsible for food inflation during the pandemic and that Kroger would raise prices at Albertsons stores.

---

[54] This section was written in July 2024, before the trial in the FTC's case against the Kroger/Albertsons merger (in August and September 2024) and its outcome (in December 2024). The Postscript includes additional perspective on the trial and decision.

- The FTC claimed that Kroger and Albertsons were the two largest grocers in the United States.

- The FTC claimed that Kroger would close stores and lay off thousands of teammates.

- The FTC claimed that unionized supermarket workers need special (unprecedented) protections to the extent they could be negatively impacted by the merger (even if it were positive for consumers).

- The FTC claimed that any sale of stores necessary to address local overlap between Kroger and Albertsons and maintain vigorous competition in certain markets (a "divestiture") would be a per se failure because some prior acquisitions of divested stores have failed, particularly the acquisition by Haggen of various stores that were divested by Albertsons when it acquired Safeway nearly a decade earlier, in 2015 (when the grocery market was materially different and far less competitive than it is today).

- The FTC claimed that C&S Wholesale Grocers, once it had agreed to acquire 413 stores (at first) — and then later 579 stores — that would be divested to address overlap in certain markets, was not capable of running the business and maintaining competition in those markets.

The disingenuous claims made by the FTC ignored the reality of how consumers shop for groceries and the extreme challenges supermarket grocers are facing as they compete with national/discount grocers like Amazon, Costco, Walmart and Aldi. In fact, I did not (and still don't) know any actual grocers who have said they thought these politicians, or the FTC, were correct in making these arguments against the Kroger/Albertsons merger. What was clear, however, was that there was a great deal of misinformation being spread across the country.

The Real Causes of Food Inflation

Food inflation from 2020 to 2024 has been incredibly difficult for American families. However, in the context of the merger, there have been widespread misperceptions and numerous misstatements about its causes. I will therefore briefly digress to address them.

In short, grocers did not cause the food inflation we have all experienced. The real causes fall into three buckets: (1) Covid and ecological supply chain disruptions; (2); Russia's invasion of Ukraine; and (3) food manufacturer price increases, including "shrinkflation."

Supply Chain Disruptions

Covid snarled the global supply chain, from manufacturing output reductions to shipping delays and countless worker absences. Ecological challenges, including extreme weather and Avian flu, meaningfully impacted the food supply. Together with widespread Covid fears and a significant amount of stimulus dollars spread across the population, these shortages sparked panic buying. All of these factors drove food inflation to 8.6 percent in February 2022, before Russia attacked Ukraine.

Numerous ecologically-driven raw material shortages (e.g., soybeans, sugar, cocoa and oranges) have also meaningfully impacted the food supply and exacerbated inflation. There have also been significant labor shortages, particularly truckers (which is why Walmart has been offering to pay truckers over $110,000 per year[55]).

---

[55] https://corporate.walmart.com/news/2022/04/07/drive-in-opportunity-walmart-raises-driver-pay-and-launches-private-fleet-development-program

Russia's Invasion of Ukraine

Before the invasion, Russia and Ukraine were responsible for roughly 30 percent of global grain and fertilizer exports. Russia is also a significant fuel exporter. When production and exports all but shut down and demand for non-Russian energy increased, there was even more food and energy cost pressure. For example, wheat prices increased 34 percent per metric ton from February 2022 to May 2022, beyond already elevated levels of supply disruption. As a result, food inflation soared, peaking at 13.5 percent in late 2022. By 2023, much of this supply had been restored, but there remained considerable volatility given continued geopolitical hostilities.

Food Manufacturer Price Increases to Grocery Customers

Here is the big one. Food manufacturers — not grocers — drive price dynamics in American grocery, from national/discount grocers like supercenters, club grocers and dollar grocers to online grocers and supermarket grocers. And food manufacturers have done very, very well in the past few years.

For example, the collective gross margin of P&G, Mondelez, Kellogg's and Coca-Cola increased over 3 percent from the middle of 2023 to 2024 — a significant dollar amount — as their company leaders openly discussed on earnings calls their continued ability to pass along price increases to customers.

FOOD MANUFACTURERS HAVE LARGELY PASSED INFLATION COSTS ONTO THEIR CONSUMERS

GROSS MARGIN EXPANSION

Company	1 Year Change
P&G	364 bps
Kellogg's	400 bps
Mondelēz International	375 bps
Coca-Cola	201 bps
Average	+335 bps

Source: Publicly available information and Capital IQ as of September 2024.
Note: Represents change from the twelve month period ending June.

Steve Cahillane, Kellogg's CEO, said in the company's Q4 2022 earnings call:

> *Our double-digit organic growth and net sales in 2022 was driven by price mix, which accelerated in the second half as we continued to execute revenue growth management actions around the world to cover accelerated input cost inflation.*

Dirk Van de Put, CEO of Mondelez, said in that company's Q2 2023 earnings call:

> *We've increased prices more aggressively… We increased prices in August, in January and another one later in Q1.*

Andre Schulten, P&G's CFO, said in P&G's Q2 2023 earnings call:

> *Pricing has been a core component of our growth for 18 out of the last 19 years.*

These challenges were aggravated by "shrinkflation," which is when food manufacturers reduce product size or quantity while still charging the same price. It is another form of food price inflation, simultaneously apparent (particularly to budget-oriented shoppers) and deceptive, in a way that makes customers feel like they are being taken advantage of.

According to Ipsos Consumer Tracking in June 2023, more than eight in ten consumers (83 percent) reported noticing that they are getting less and paying the same amount or more, and nearly as many (79 percent) said they felt cheated when it happened.[56]

SHRINKFLATION BY FOOD MANUFACTURERS MAKES CONSUMERS FEEL CHEATED

Shrinkflation Examples (Prices Remained Constant)

16oz ➤ 14oz   19.3oz ➤ 18.1oz   9.75oz ➤ 9.25oz   32oz ➤ 28oz

Mondelēz International   General Mills   PEPSICO

"We took just a little bit out of the [Doritos] bag so we can give you the same price..."
– Frito-Lay spokesperson

Source: Supermarket News, Business Insider, Ipsos Consumer Tracker and Forbes

These were the ***actual*** dynamics that drove grocery price inflation across the country. Supermarket grocers could not control them because they do not

---

[56] Ipsos Consumer Tracking (06/12/2023) https://www.ipsos.com/en-us/americans-are-noticing-shrinkflation-and-theyre-not-happy

have the low cost-of-capital flexibility required to absorb these costs like larger national/discount grocers. Food inflation was therefore well beyond what smaller grocers could absorb and remain profitable without passing it along.

Some politicians and the FTC have repeatedly attempted to scapegoat grocers with a misguided and inaccurate effort to call food inflation something far worse, price gouging, which is illegal.

While surely there were some immoral fringe actors who criminally violated price gouging laws during the pandemic (who should most certainly be prosecuted for their crimes, consistent with many longstanding state laws), Leslie Sarasin, CEO of FMI, articulated the important distinction with crystal clarity:

> *"It is inaccurate and irresponsible to conflate an illegal activity like price gouging ... with inflation, which is a broad, macroeconomic measure of increases in consumer prices over time due to supply chain cost pressures.... When discussing food prices, it is imperative that our conversations remain grounded in reality and data, rather than rhetoric."*[57]

[57] https://www.fmi.org/newsroom/news-archive/view/2024/08/15/fmi-statement-on-misconceptions-about-food-price-inflation-and-industry-practices

COVID, SUPPLY CHAIN CHALLENGES, UKRAINE AND FOOD MANUFACTURERS DROVE FOOD INFLATION (NOT GROCERS)

CPI FOOD AT HOME

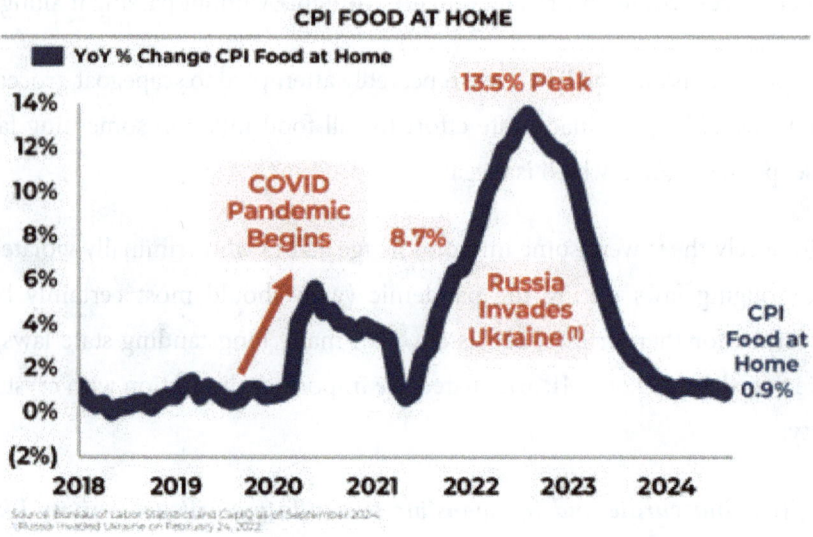

Why Kroger/Albertsons Would Be Fair, Necessary and Good for America

My team and I were engaged by Albertsons soon after the transaction was announced to help educate the market on the current realities of American grocery, how drastically it has changed over the years and the reasons why the merger would be good for customers, teammates and communities.

I conducted several dozen industry briefings with different constituencies from across the country, with dozens of press interviews, including TV appearances on Bloomberg, Fox Business and Yahoo Finance. I wrote a bunch of op-eds and published a series of infographic articles called *"5 Things You Might Not Know"* about each of Walmart, Costco, Amazon, Target, Aldi and Dollar General. Over time, the more general industry education effort evolved into somewhat incisively enumerating the reasons why I thought the FTC was just plain wrong.

For starters, let's look at where Kroger and Albertsons operate. They have very complementary footprints. Albertsons is mostly in the Northeast, the Mountains and West Coast; Kroger is mostly in the Midwest and Southeast, with some presence in western states as well. To maintain strong competition, mostly in western states, C&S would be buying 579 stores being divested by Albertsons.

KROGER / ALBERTSONS: COMPLEMENTARY FOOTPRINT WITH ICONIC AND TRUSTED SUPERMARKET BANNERS

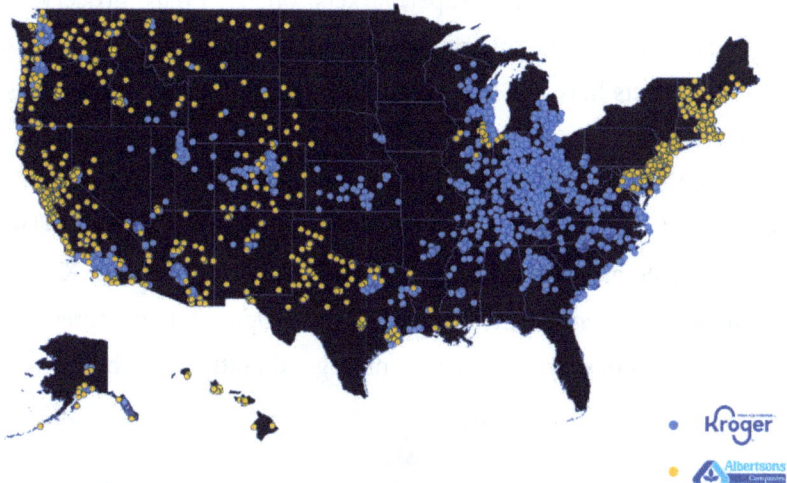

There are four clear reasons why I argued this transaction would be fair, necessary and good for the country:

#1 – The 2024 grocery market is far more diverse and competitive than the 1980s grocery market the FTC describes.

#2 – Kroger has a long track record of better prices and better wages, and made clear commitments to improve prices and wages even more with the Albertsons acquisition.

#3 – The grocery labor market is very fluid; it's not a rigid, monolithic group of unionized supermarket workers.

#4 – C&S would become a leading grocery retailer, poised to maintain competition across divestiture markets.

#1. The 2024 grocery market is far more diverse and competitive than the 1980s grocery market the FTC describes.

The grocery market in 2024 is far more diverse and competitive than the contrived, gerrymandered, "supermarkets only," 1980s grocery market described by the FTC and other complaints in Colorado and Washington. We all know the facts here. As I noted earlier, the average American household regularly shops at over five grocers. Just ask your friends, families or colleagues; they all likely shop at Walmart, Target, Costco, Amazon/Whole Foods, Aldi/Trader Joe's, Dollar General and/or Family Dollar/Dollar Tree. Walmart's U.S grocery sales are more than twice that of Kroger and Albertsons **combined**, particularly net of the proposed divestitures. Costco's U.S. grocery business is over 50 percent larger than that of Albertsons.

WALMART'S U.S. GROCERY SALES ARE TWICE KROGER / ALBERTSONS COMBINED; COSTCO HAS 50% MORE U.S. GROCERY SALES THAN ALBERTSONS

WALMART VS. KROGER + ALBERTSONS	COSTCO VS. ALBERTSONS

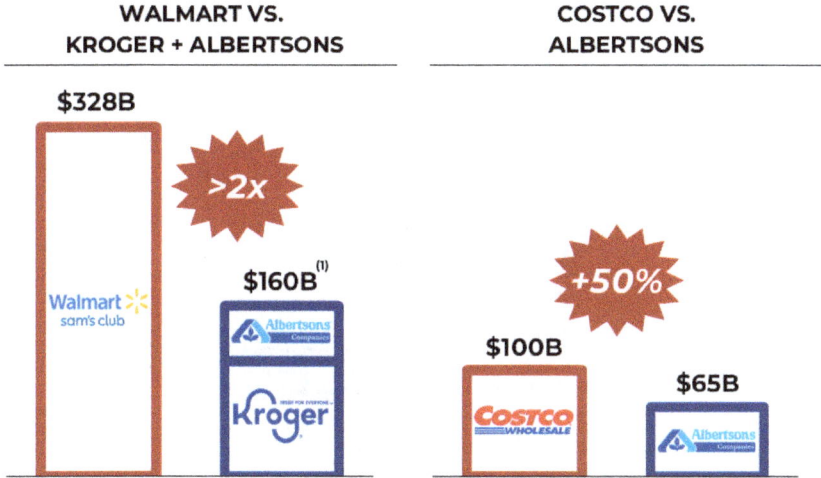

$328B — Walmart, sam's club

>2x

$160B [1] — Albertsons / Kroger

+50%

$100B — Costco Wholesale

$65B — Albertsons

Source: Company filings and Capital IQ as of September 2024.
Note: Reflects annual U.S. grocery sales, excluding pharmacy, fuel and other non-grocery categories.
1) Reflects estimated sales of 579 stores being sold to C&S.

On the West Coast — where most of the overlap between Kroger and Albertsons is located — there are dozens of exceptional grocery competitors. Consumers have numerous grocery choices, including Sprouts, Natural Grocers, Stater Bros., Bristol Farms/New Seasons/Metropolitan Market (Good Food Holdings), Gelson's, Mother's Markets, Raley's/Bashas'/AJ's Finer Foods/Food City (all owned by Raley's since 2021), Smart & Final/El Super (owned by Mexico's Grupo Chedraui), Northgate, Vallarta, Cardenas/Los Altos Ranch (owned by Heritage Grocers), Grocery Outlet, WinCo, 99 Ranch, Hmart and many others.

Saying Costco, Amazon/Whole Foods, Aldi, Trader Joe's and Sprouts aren't grocers is just not a defensible argument in 2024, particularly since it would suggest that these grocers don't vigorously compete every day with supermarket grocers for customers and teammates, which is just absurd.

WEST COAST GROCERY IS HIGHLY COMPETITIVE

In the 10 years from 2012 to 2022, the national/discount grocers added 1,600 stores on the West Coast, particularly Grocery Outlet, Walmart, Target, WinCo, the dollar grocers, Aldi, Trader Joe's and Costco.

NATIONAL / DISCOUNT GROCERS HAVE TRANSFORMED GROCERY

WEST COAST STORE COUNT CHANGE (2012-2022)

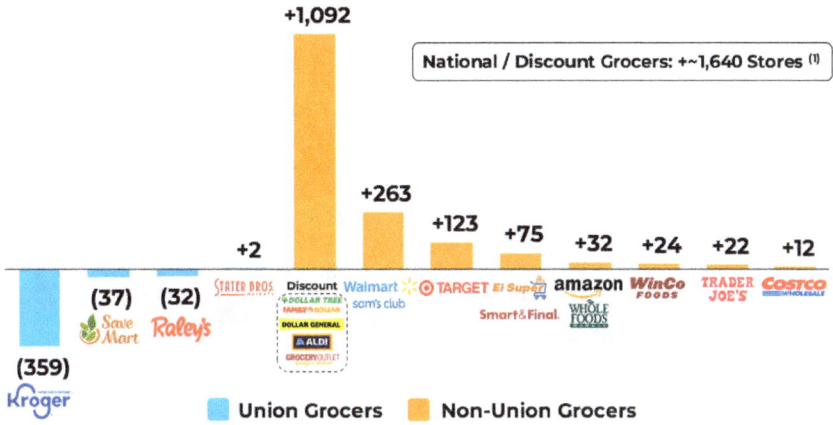

National / Discount Grocers: +~1,640 Stores [1]

+1,092

+263

+123

+75

+32

+24

+22

+12

+2

(37)   (32)

(359)

Union Grocers   **Non-Union Grocers**

Source: Chain Store Guide ("CSG") Grocery Market Share Studies.
Note: Store count and share data consists of data from core-based statistical area across the US. Does not include online grocery fulfilled outside of stores. CBSAs ranked according to total Kroger & Albertsons store count. 2012 CSG data was adjusted to reflect 2022 parent company and sub-banner relationships where possible.
[1]Total combined store count change for Walmart, Amazon / Whole Foods, Target, Costco, Smart & Final, WinCo, Trader Joe's and Discount operators across the West Coast (AZ, CA, NV, OR, WA).

On the West Coast, Walmart is the #1 grocer and Costco is #2, which is a big shift from 10 years ago, when they were #4 and #3, respectively. Their combined market share actually increased more than 50 percent since 2012. To be fair, back then, Albertsons (including Safeway) and Kroger were #1 and #2, respectively; but they have since lost roughly a third of their combined share.

NATIONAL / DISCOUNT GROCERS' GROWTH HAS COME LARGELY AT THE EXPENSE OF SUPERMARKET GROCERS

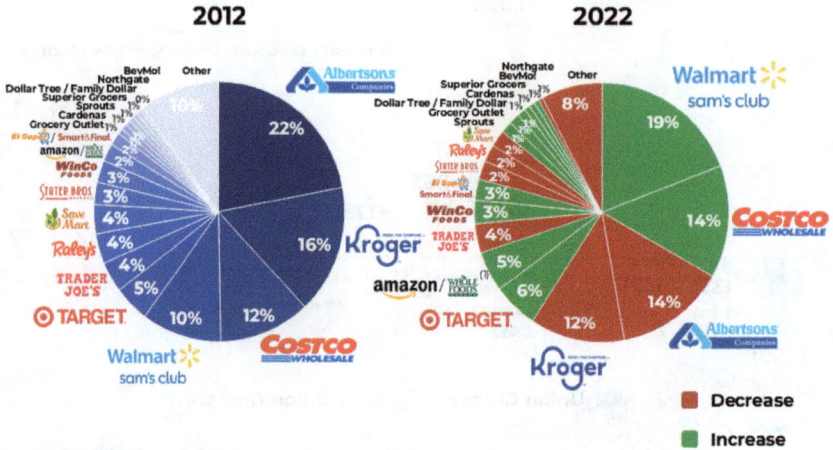

WEST COAST GROCERY SHARE CHANGE (2012-2022)

Source: Chain Store Guide ("CSG") Grocery Market Share Studies and eMarketer.
1) Includes estimated online grocery sales of Amazon / Whole Foods. Assumes online grocery penetration in the market equivalent to the population of the market as a % of the U.S.

To be more specific, over the last 10 years, Walmart's West Coast market share is up 9 percent, Amazon/Whole Foods is up 3 percent, and Costco is up 2 percent. Each of Target, Smart & Final and WinCo added share as well.

In sum, the national/discount grocers have added 18 percent market share on the West Coast, while Kroger & Albertsons lost 12 percent share. Other supermarket grocers lost share as well.

NATIONAL / DISCOUNT GROCERS' GROWTH HAS COME LARGELY AT THE EXPENSE OF SUPERMARKET GROCERS (CONT'D)

WEST COAST GROCERY SHARE CHANGE (2012-2022)

National / Discount Grocers: +18% Share (1)

+9% Walmart / sam's club (0%)
+3% amazon(2) / WHOLE FOODS
+2% Costco WHOLESALE
+2% Discount — DOLLAR TREE, FAMILY DOLLAR, DOLLAR GENERAL, ALDI, GROCERY OUTLET
+1% TARGET
+1% El Super / Smart & Final
+0% WinCo FOODS
(0%) TRADER JOE'S
(2%) Raley's
(2%) Save Mart
(12%) Kroger / Albertsons

■ Union Grocers ■ Non-Union Grocers

Source: Chain Store Guide ("CSG") Grocery Market Share Studies.
Note: Store count and share data consists of data from core-based statistical area across the US. Does not include online grocery fulfilled outside of stores. CBSAs ranked according to total Kroger & Albertsons store count. 2012 CSG data was adjusted to reflect 2022 parent company and sub-banner relationships where possible.
1) Total combined % share change for Walmart, Amazon / Whole Foods, Target, Smart & Final, Costco, WinCo and Trader Joe's and Discount operators across the West Coast (AZ, CA, NV, OR, WA).
2) Includes estimated online grocery sales of Amazon / Whole Foods. Assumes online grocery penetration in the market equivalent to the population of the market as a % of the U.S.

Finally, non-union grocers added nearly 20 percent share, capturing nearly two-thirds of the total, with 30 percent more share than unionized grocers.

WEST COAST UNIONIZED GROCERS ARE LOSING SHARE TO NON-UNION NATIONAL / DISCOUNT GROCERS

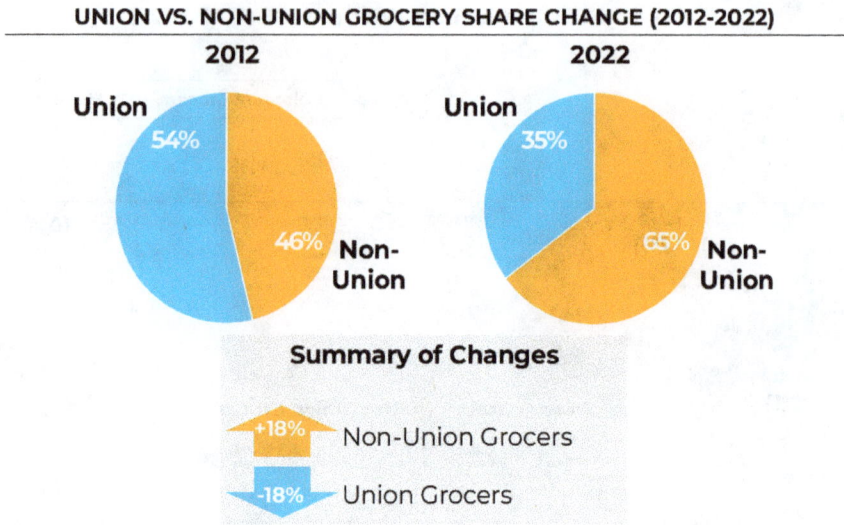

UNION VS. NON-UNION GROCERY SHARE CHANGE (2012-2022)

2012

Union

54%

46% **Non-Union**

2022

Union

35%

65% **Non-Union**

Summary of Changes

+18% Non-Union Grocers

-18% Union Grocers

Note: Excludes other grocers with <0.5% share.

#2. Kroger has a long track record of better prices and better wages, and made clear commitments to improve prices and wages even more with the Albertsons acquisition.

The key question for America on the Kroger/Albertsons merger is the impact it would have on customers, teammates and communities. Kroger made some extraordinary public commitments — both in interviews with CEO Rodney McMullen and in numerous company statements — that with the acquisition, the company would invest billions of dollars to lower prices, raise wages and improve stores, which would both strengthen and protect union jobs.

Kroger committed to invest $1 billion in better prices, starting day one (up from their original commitment of $500 million). They promised there would be no store closures and no front-line job losses related to the merger. They would assume all union collective bargaining agreements, which have industry-leading healthcare and pension benefits. They would invest $1 billion for better wages and $1.3 billion for better stores, which would strengthen the jobs in those stores. They would extend their $21,000 tuition reimbursement program to full-time and part-time Albertsons employees. To combat food insecurity, they would donate 10 billion meals by 2030 — that's enough to feed every person in Boston, Chicago, Denver and Seattle, every meal, every day, for nearly two years.

KROGER'S CLEAR PUBLIC COMMITMENTS RELATED TO THE ALBERTSONS MERGER

Kroger's Clear Commitments

- $1 Billion for better prices, <u>starting Day One.</u>
  - Building on Kroger's $5 billion better price track record in last 20 years
- No store closures
- No front-line job losses
- Assuming all collective bargaining agreements
  - With industry-leading healthcare and pension benefits
- $1 Billion for better wages
  - Building on Kroger's $2.4 billion wage improvement track record since 2018
- $1.3 Billion for better stores
- $21,000 tuition reimbursement for full-time and part-time employees
- Donating 10 billion meals to combat food insecurity

Why is all of this credible?

Well, lowering prices is literally Kroger's business model. Kroger has an exceptional, 20-year track record of better prices and wages, both company-wide and with acquisitions they've made. They've invested $5 billion in better prices over that period, consistently lowering the company's gross margin over many years. But for these investments, Kroger's customers would have paid billions more in higher grocery prices.

KROGER'S BUSINESS IS BUILT ON REDUCING COSTS TO ATTRACT CUSTOMERS AND BUILD LOYALTY

Kroger

CLEAR TRACK RECORD OF GROSS MARGIN REDUCTION DEMONSTRATES KROGER'S COMMITMENT TO LOWER PRICES FOR THEIR CUSTOMERS

TOTAL GROSS MARGIN DECLINE YOY

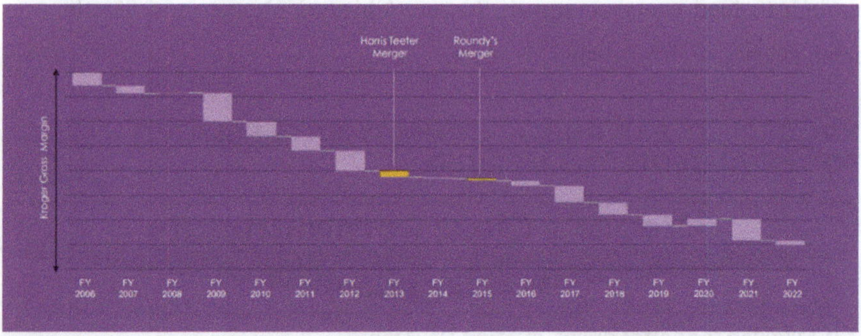

Kroger customers would be paying billions in higher prices if Kroger had maintained rather than reduced its gross margin rate from 2005

Source: Stakeholders Fact Sheet, November 10, 2022, krogeralbertsons.com/resources.

Kroger has made these margin investments both company-wide and at acquired companies. When Kroger acquired Harris Teeter, they invested over $125 million in better prices; when they acquired Roundy's, they invested over $100 million. In both cases, they intentionally brought their gross profit margin down materially to deliver more value for their customers, which strengthened stores, and the jobs in those stores.

KROGER LOWERED PRICES AT HARRIS TEETER AND ROUNDY'S AFTER MERGERS

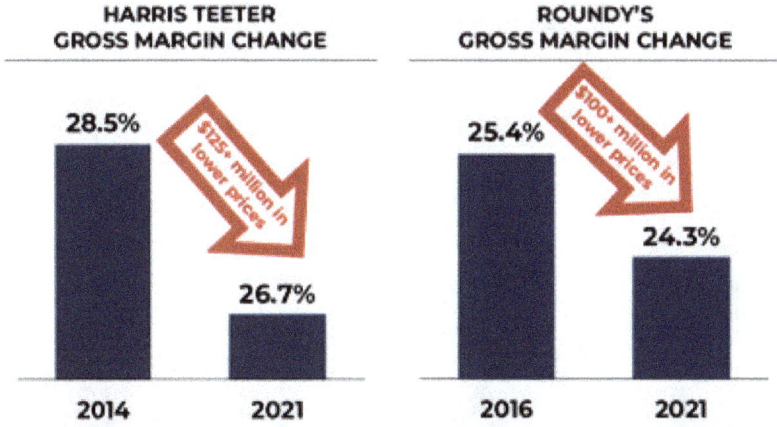

HARRIS TEETER GROSS MARGIN CHANGE

28.5% → 26.7%

$125+ million in lower prices

2014 — 2021

ROUNDY'S GROSS MARGIN CHANGE

25.4% → 24.3%

$100+ million in lower prices

2016 — 2021

Kroger has invested more than $125 million to lower prices at Harris Teeter and more than $100 million to lower prices at Roundy's

Over the past 20 years, Kroger has intentionally reduced its company-wide gross profit margin by 5 percent — an extraordinary amount — in order to provide better prices for consumers, while margins at Amazon, Walmart, Ahold Delhaize and Dollar General have all increased.

WHILE MANY GROCERS HAVE INCREASED THEIR GROSS MARGINS, KROGER HAS REDUCED THEIRS TO LOWER PRICES FOR CONSUMERS

20-YEAR GROSS MARGIN CHANGE

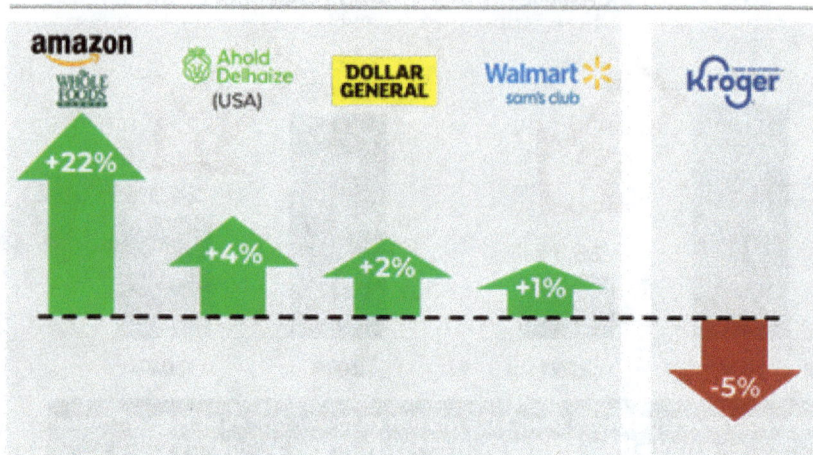

Source: Company filings through 2023.

#3. The grocery labor market is very fluid; it's not a rigid, monolithic group of unionized supermarket workers

We have established that most grocery jobs today are at non-union grocers, not unionized supermarket grocers like Kroger and Albertsons. While unionized grocery jobs have declined precipitously across the country, Kroger has added over 110,000 union jobs in the past twenty years.

The FTC has suggested — in a literally unprecedented claim — that transactions should be evaluated not only on the impact on consumers (price), but also on the impact on labor. They have suggested the transaction should be rejected because labor unions will have one less party with whom to negotiate better wages and benefits, and that unionized supermarket grocery employees are a discrete type of workers that require artificial protections beyond the fluid labor market.

As I noted above, I have been a staunch supporter of America's grocery teammates for a long time, but it's important to focus on the facts. Turnover at supermarket grocers is very high, mainly because these grocers compete every day for employees with thousands of companies offering millions of jobs. These other companies include non-union grocers (like Walmart, Target, Costco and Amazon, which as noted earlier, account for most grocery jobs today); gig workers (like Door Dash, Instacart and Uber); restaurants (with over 11 million jobs at over 700,000 establishments); hotels; and non-food retailers (like Gap, Home Depot, Ulta, Foot Locker or Macy's).

SUPERMARKET GROCERS COMPETE FOR TEAMMATES WITH THOUSANDS OF COMPANIES EMPLOYING MILLIONS OF PEOPLE

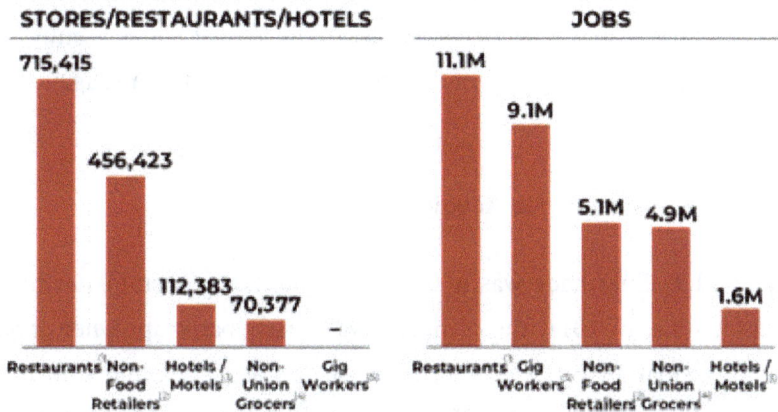

STORES/RESTAURANTS/HOTELS

715,415 — Restaurants
456,423 — Non-Food Retailers
112,383 — Hotels / Motels
70,377 — Non-Union Grocers
— Gig Workers

JOBS

11.1M — Restaurants
9.1M — Gig Workers
5.1M — Non-Food Retailers
4.9M — Non-Union Grocers
1.6M — Hotels / Motels

It is also important to remember that union employees at larger, stronger grocers usually get better wages and benefits than at smaller, weaker grocers that can't afford them.

While grocery teammates are the salt of the earth and part of the very fabric of our country, and have proven themselves to be counted among the most essential and indispensable workers in America, the FTC's mandate is to protect *consumers*. Workers are protected by the National Labor Relations Board, not the FTC.

All things being equal, higher costs mean higher prices for consumers at the checkout line. We can't have it both ways as a society if we want supermarket grocers to continue to serve our communities in the long run.

#4. C&S would become a leading grocery retailer, poised to maintain competition across divestiture markets.

The key thesis in the FTC's argument against C&S as the divestiture buyer has been that because (nearly a decade ago) a very small grocer called Haggen failed in its acquisition of stores that were divested out of Albertsons/Safeway, C&S — one of the largest grocery companies in the United States — must not be capable of running a business of divested stores well today. Yet again, let's go through the facts.

Haggen's (Inapposite) Failed Acquisition

Haggen Food & Pharmacy was a small supermarket grocer in northwest Washington state. In 2011, the company was nearly bankrupt when it was acquired by a small private equity firm focused on acquiring and lending to distressed companies. By 2014, Haggen had shrunk from 32 stores to 18 stores. It then acquired 146 stores divested by Albertsons and Safeway, a business that was eight times its size. Most of these stores were in southern California, Arizona and Nevada, where Haggen did not operate; but Haggen was required to immediately convert — at closing — each of the Albertsons and Safeway stores to the Haggen banner, which customers did not know. Haggen's very small size and limited capital capacity made it difficult for the company to invest in better prices, sufficient marketing or the team required to successfully compete. Customers were confused — in some of the most competitive grocery markets in the United States. As a result of these challenges, sales, cash flow and liquidity dropped precipitously, and Haggen filed for bankruptcy in late 2015.[58]

C&S Is Nothing Like Haggen

C&S is a radically different company than Haggen, for a bunch of powerful reasons. First, C&S is a $20+ billion grocery business that is *over 40 times larger* than Haggen was. C&S is the 8th-largest private company in America, supplying over 7,500 independent grocery stores — with a broad network of dozens of distribution centers — across the country.

C&S is family-owned (not owned by private equity), with a 100-year, successful track record operating as a leading grocery merchant. C&S is a well-capitalized buyer, with extensive infrastructure across the country. C&S has a strong balance sheet to support customers, jobs and store investments, which is how you compete in grocery.

C&S has an exceptional management team, with extensive acquisition and integration experience. Albertsons' COO, Susan Morris, who is one of America's most respected grocery executives, would be CEO of C&S Retail.

C&S agreed to spend $2.9 billion to expand its retail footprint, which is a critical evolution of their long-term strategy to complement their wholesale heritage. They clearly did this with an intention to be successful with their investment.

---

[58] In full disclosure, I worked on various transactions with Haggen in different roles over several years. I led the sale in 2011 (along with then-CEO Jim Donald, who turned around the company well enough for us to be able to salvage a sale). I sold the Haggen family's real estate in 2012 (preserving a significant portion of the value of the family's overall asset portfolio). We introduced Albertsons' owners to Haggen's owners in 2014 and were tangentially involved, in an unusually limited way, in the divestiture acquisition. After Haggen went into bankruptcy, we were hired again by Haggen to sell the company's stores, which ultimately were acquired by over a dozen buyers, including Gelson's, Smart & Final, Sprouts, Stater Bros. and 99 Ranch, but also including Albertsons (which the FTC permitted to re-acquire any stores that had no other interest from other buyers).

In a significant departure from the Haggen transaction, C&S would be buying or licensing various local store banners in order to maintain customer continuity, loyalty and performance. It would be acquiring Carrs in Alaska; QFC and Haggen in the Northwest and Mariano's in Illinois. It would be licensing the Safeway banner in Colorado and Arizona and the Albertsons banner in California and Wyoming. Only a relatively small percentage of the stores it would be acquiring would need to be rebannered with store names that are not already operating and known in the market, and those conversions would happen over an extended period to ensure stability with customers.

Furthermore, C&S was actually validated by the FTC as a divestiture buyer just two-plus years earlier in the Price Chopper/Tops merger in upstate New York (on which I advised Price Chopper). C&S acquired 12 stores that the FTC required the companies to divest.

COMPARING C&S WHOLESALE GROCERS TO HAGGEN IS INCORRECT ON MULTIPLE LEVELS

THE DISTINCT CHARACTERISTICS THAT LED TO THE FAILURE OF HAGGEN'S ACQUISITION OF DIVESTED STORES IN 2015 ARE NOT PRESENT WITH C&S WHOLESALE GROCERS TODAY

HAGGEN (2015)	C&S WHOLESALE GROCERS (2024)
✗ Nearly bankrupt just a few years before acquired divestiture stores	✓ Strong, well-capitalized buyer with solid 104-year operating / integration track record
✗ Very small chain owned by a small private equity firm	✓ One of the largest private companies in the U.S.; ~$20 billion in sales and ample financial investment capacity; serves 7,500 grocery stores across U.S.
✗ Haggen banner was unknown to customers in the new markets where they changed banner and re-opened stores as Haggen	✓ C&S buying / licensing local banners (Carrs, QFC, Haggen and Mariano's, plus Safeway / Albertsons in some markets) to maintain continuity, customer loyalty and performance
✗ Haggen's weak balance sheet led to insufficient capital invested to build brand recognition	✓ Robust balance sheet and infrastructure to support customers, jobs and store investments
✗ Haggen's senior management team lacked local operating and integration experience	✓ Experienced management team with extensive acquisition and integration experience (as an approved FTC divestiture buyer just two years ago)

Perhaps most important, C&S would be assuming union collective bargaining agreements. Bear in mind that these stores could have been sold to a non-union buyer, or to an anti-union grocer like Amazon. This is probably why — notwithstanding various local unions' statements against it — the transaction was endorsed by Local 555, a union representing 18,000 members in Washington, Oregon, Idaho and Wyoming, and Local 555 made this point in its endorsement of the C&S acquisition.[59]

When one couples C&S' existing store footprint and the 579 stores being acquired with its extensive supply footprint, it is clear that C&S would have a significant position in some of the largest grocery markets in the U.S., including Seattle, Portland, Los Angeles, San Diego, Las Vegas, Phoenix, Denver, Dallas, Chicago and Washington, D.C.

---

[59] Local 555 curiously withdrew its endorsement of the C&S transaction just before the Kroger/Albertsons trial began, while embroiled in a labor contract extension negotiation with Kroger.

C&S' ACQUISITION OF DIVESTED STORES WILL CREATE A STRONG GROCERY PRESENCE IN SEVERAL OF THE MOST SIGNIFICANT MARKETS IN THE U.S.

C&S RETAIL EXPANSION COMPLEMENTS ITS LEADING WHOLESALE BUSINESS THAT SERVES OVER 7,500 GROCERY CUSTOMERS WITH DOZENS OF DISTRIBUTION CENTERS ACROSS THE U.S.

Assets Being Acquired by C&S
- 579 stores from 15 different banners; includes any associated fuel centers and pharmacies
- 6 distribution centers and 1 dairy plant
- Carrs, QFC, Haggen and Mariano's banner names [1]
- Licensing Albertsons Banner in California and Wyoming and Safeway Banner in Arizona and Colorado

- Stores C&S Acquiring (579)
- DCs C&S Acquiring (6)
- Dairy Plant C&S Acquiring (1)
- Current C&S Retail Stores (165) [2]
- Current C&S DCs (36)

1) Stores currently under these banners that are retained by Kroger will be re-bannered into one of the retained Kroger or Albertsons Cos. banners following the close of the transaction.
2) C&S Retail includes ~120 franchised stores.

C&S Parallel to SpartanNash

C&S's hybrid wholesale/retail strategy is very much like SpartanNash, another multibillion-dollar grocer (publicly traded: SPTN) that supplies over 2,000 grocery stores and also operates over 100 grocery stores under ten different banners, across nine states.

SpartanNash's CEO Tony Sarsam recently made very clear in an investor conference the symbiotic relationship between grocery supply and retail, the differentiation it generates and how critical this hybrid approach is to the company's success:

> *[Retail and Wholesale] are really and truly complementary businesses. … We learn things in the retail space that we can share with our customers… gives us a competitive advantage as we share those ideas and those learnings with them. … Our retail is not a hobby, it is a big*

business [that] we have scaled, actually invested in. … So compared to other wholesale, we think this gives us a really, really interesting advantage.[60]

SPARTANNASH IS ANOTHER HYBRID GROCERY WHOLESALER WITH A VERY STRONG COMPLEMENTARY RETAIL BUSINESSES

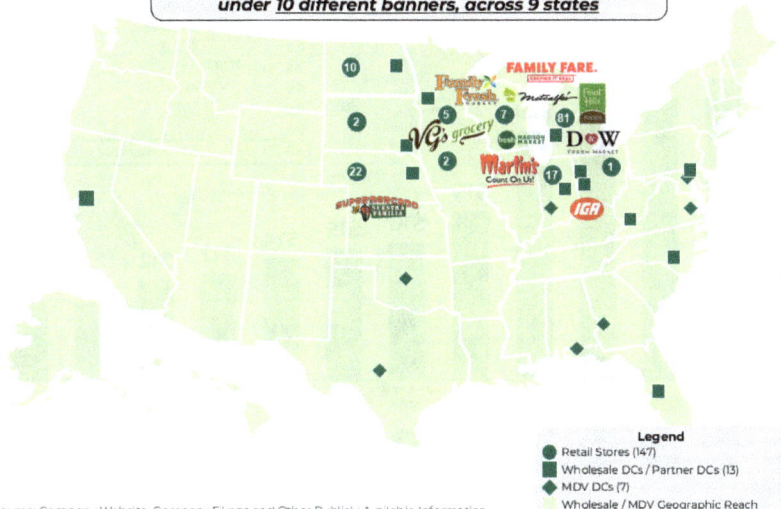

SpartanNash supplies over 2,000 grocery stores, but also owns and operates 147 retail grocery stores under 10 different banners, across 9 states

Legend
- Retail Stores (147)
- Wholesale DCs / Partner DCs (13)
- MDV DCs (7)
- Wholesale / MDV Geographic Reach

Source: Company Website, Company Filings and Other Publicly Available Information.
Note: DCs in San Antonio, TX and Columbus, GA service both the Wholesale and MDV segments. DC in Stockton, CA is operated in partnership with Coastal Pacific Food Distributors.

When the dust settled, C&S would be the #8 U.S. grocer in total sales, with over $40 billion in combined retail and wholesale grocery sales, just behind Publix but ahead of HEB and another major U.S. grocery supplier, United Natural Foods. It would be roughly five times the size of the very successful SpartanNash.

C&S's huge grocery supply business would help lower prices for customers and enhance wages for teammates to improve store experience. The larger retail business — on top of the roughly 160 stores C&S either operates or franchises — would strengthen its supply business, which would then serve

---

[60] SpartanNash Analyst/Investor Day, November 2, 2022.

over 8,000 stores across the country, almost twice as many as Kroger and Albertsons combined (4,400 stores).

AFTER ACQUIRING 579 KROGER/ALBERTSONS STORES, C&S WOULD BE THE #8 U.S. GROCER IN TOTAL SALES (RETAIL + WHOLESALE)

($ In Billions)   **TOTAL GROCERY SALES (RETAIL + WHOLESALE)**

Rank	Company	Total Grocery Sales
#1	Walmart / sam's club	$328
#2	Kroger / Albertsons	$160
#3	Costco Wholesale	$100
#4	amazon / Whole Foods Market	$67
#5	Target	$56
#6	Ahold Delhaize	$51
#7	Publix	$48
#8	C&S (Retail + Wholesale)	$43

Bar chart values ($ In Billions):

C&S Wholesale Grocers (Retail + WS)	#8	$43
H-E-B	#9	$34
Dollar General	#10	$32
UNFI (Retail + WS)	#11	$30
ALDI	#12	$29
Dollar Tree / Family Dollar	#13	$19
Trader Joe's	#14	$16
meijer	#15	$15
BJ's	#16	$14
HyVee	#17	$12
Wegmans	#18	$12
WinCo Foods	#19	$9
SpartanNash (Retail + WS)	#20	$9

Note: Pro Forma C&S Retail grocery sales reflect Solomon estimates.

C&S would be the #11th-ranked U.S. retail grocer by sales, more than Trader Joe's, BJ's Sprouts, and some storied grocers like Meijer, Hy-Vee, Wegman's, WinCo, Giant Eagle and DeMoulas Market Basket.

C&S WOULD BE THE #11 U.S. GROCERY RETAILER, WITH MORE RETAIL GROCERY SALES THAN MANY SIGNIFICANT U.S. GROCERS

($ In Billions)   **U.S. RETAIL GROCERY SALES**

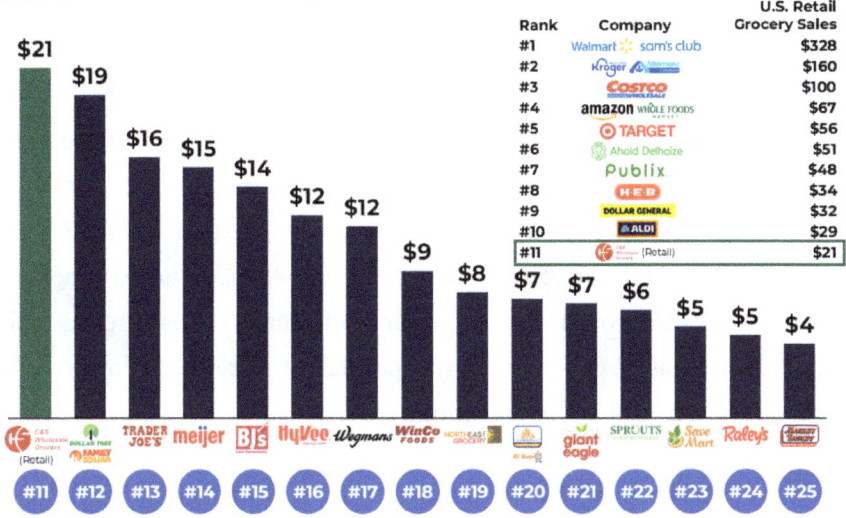

Rank	Company	U.S. Retail Grocery Sales
#1	Walmart sam's club	$328
#2	Kroger	$160
#3	Costco	$100
#4	amazon WHOLE FOODS	$67
#5	TARGET	$56
#6	Ahold Delhaize	$51
#7	Publix	$48
#8	H-E-B	$34
#9	DOLLAR GENERAL	$32
#10	ALDI	$29
#11	(Retail)	$21

Bar chart values: $21, $19, $16, $15, $14, $12, $12, $9, $8, $7, $7, $6, $5, $5, $4

| #11 | #12 | #13 | #14 | #15 | #16 | #17 | #18 | #19 | #20 | #21 | #22 | #23 | #24 | #25 |

Note: Pro Forma C&S Retail grocery sales reflect Solomon estimates.

C&S would be ranked #9 by number of stores, more than Costco, Amazon/Whole Foods, Trader Joe's, Grocery Outlet, Sprouts, HEB, Hy-Vee, Meijer and Giant Eagle, as well as public grocers like Ingles Markets and Weis Markets.

There have been suggestions that notwithstanding the nearly $3 billion cost (including a material amount from the Cohen family), the herculean effort that C&S expended throughout the transaction to be positioned to acquire these stores and the considerable capital it expects it would invest once it did, that C&S does not intend to keep stores open and would seek some pretext to close stores following the transaction. This would be completely irrational, as it would cause C&S to lose both supply volume and retail profit, in other words, the diametric opposite of its strategy. It would also be a terrible investment for the Cohen family.

In short, Kroger/Albertsons would be good for America, if the court were willing to see present day grocery reality.

* * *

After America's supermarket grocers stepped up to feed their nearly locked-down communities during the pandemic and since we emerged from it, it is surprising there still is not more clear recognition among regulators of the critical role that supermarket grocers play serving customers in crisis after crisis, the existential challenges they face, and the consumer benefits of enabling them to grow and become more efficient. The fact remains that without more scale to compete, many supermarket grocers may not be around in the next crisis to help feed our communities.

Enter the Ghost of Supermarkets Future.

CHAPTER 8

The Ghost of Supermarkets Future

When you add up all of these grocery facts, the key implications are unfortunately very clear:

#1. Supermarket grocers are a shrinking part of a much larger U.S. grocery landscape

#2. There's more grocery choice, convenience, competition and price transparency than ever before

#3. Just like department stores before them, supermarket grocers are under siege from national/discount operators

#4. Millions of jobs – especially union jobs – are at risk, as is the deeply important place supermarket grocers hold as pillars of thousands of American communities

The logical extension of the trajectory of Supermarkets Present is not dissimilar to that of America's department store sector. Looking back 30-plus years ago, there were dozens of department store chains across the country, many of which were family-owned.

U.S. DEPARTMENT STORE LANDSCAPE, 1990 VS. CURRENT

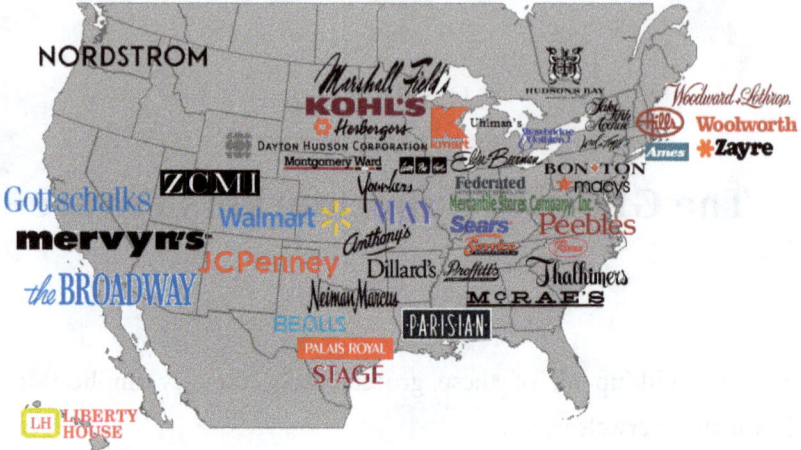

Source: Company filings and websites, news articles and Wall Street Research.

Over the past few decades, most regional department store chains have been rationalized by the rise of the same national/discount operators — Walmart, Target, Costco and Amazon — along with other online retailers and numerous specialty operators. As a result, there were many department store bankruptcies, including Sears and Kmart, two of the leading chains for decades.

RAPID GROWTH AND EXTREME COMPETITIVE PRESSURE FROM LARGE, UBIQUITOUS NATIONAL, DISCOUNT, ONLINE AND SPECIALTY RETAILERS HAS CAUSED MANY DEPARTMENT STORE BANKRUPTCIES

RECENT DEPARTMENT STORE BANKRUPTCIES

Sears	Neiman Marcus	JCPenney	Kmart
belk	BON·TON Your Store. Your Style.	BARNEYS NEW YORK	GOTTSCHALKS
Stein Mart	Century 21	ZCMI	the BROADWAY
Lord & Taylor	Peebles your town. your store.	bealls OUTLET	Woolworth
mervyns California	STAGE	OLYMPIA Sports	Ames

There are only a few department store chains left today. Those that have survived were generally supported by significant combinations, which brought sufficient scale, better credit ratings and lower-cost capital. This provided these department store chains the operating flexibility needed to make the investments required to continue to compete.

One good example is the merger of the former consolidators Federated and May Companies, which merged in 2005 to become Macy's. While their performance has not always been consistent in an increasingly difficult competitive environment, it is undeniable that Macy's has been able to continue to evolve and maintain some degree of relevance to consumers.

169

U.S. DEPARTMENT STORE LANDSCAPE, 1990 VS. CURRENT

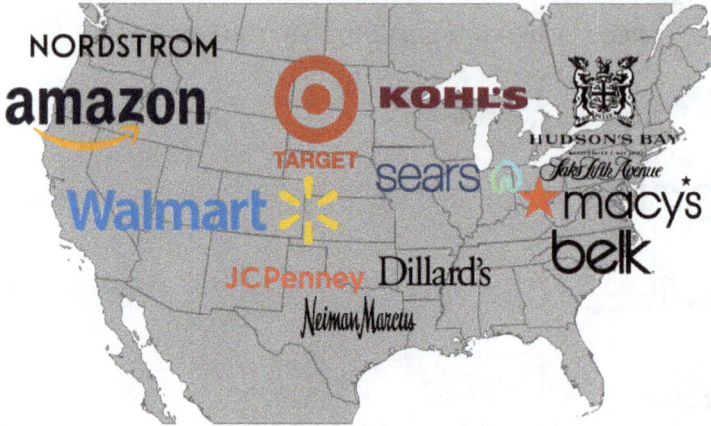

Source: Company filings and websites, news articles and Wall Street Research.

Similar dynamics have been at work in the grocery industry. The shift from Supermarkets Past to Supermarkets Present has forced many supermarket grocers to close stores and many supermarket teammates to lose their jobs. This is the fate we assign to the good folks who, in crisis after crisis, are always the last to leave and the first ones back in, the unsung heroes who are always there for us.

Supermarket grocers in American grocery today look very much like department stores did in general merchandise a few decades ago. The industry is as fragmented as ever, with hundreds of grocers operating thousands of grocery stores all across the country while building ubiquitous online grocery businesses.

Like department stores, there is a long list of national/discount, online and specialty operators who are continuously taking share.

U.S. GROCERY STORE LANDSCAPE, CURRENT VS. FUTURE

CURRENT

Source: Company filings and websites, news articles and Wall Street Research.

And like department stores, supermarket grocers have unfortunately also endured a long series of bankruptcies in the past few years. From A&P (the Walmart of the 1950s and 1960s) twice (in 2010 and 2015), to Bashas', Homeland, C&K Markets, and many others, including Winn-Dixie (also twice, once when it was a family-owned grocer in 2005 and again when owned by Southeastern Grocers, in 2018). Aldi just acquired Winn-Dixie in early 2024, which suggests it is unlikely there will be a third Winn-Dixie bankruptcy.

NUMEROUS SMALLER GROCERS HAVE BEEN RATIONALIZED BY RAPID GROWTH AND EXTREME COMPETITIVE PRESSURE FROM LARGE, UBIQUITOUS NATIONAL / DISCOUNT GROCERS

RECENT GROCERY BANKRUPTCIES

As each day passes, national/discount grocers gain momentum in the zero-sum battle for sustainable customer loyalty, along with the revenue, EBITDA and shareholder value it brings, particularly as online grocery penetration grows in the next few years.

With Amazon projected to meaningfully increase its market share in the next decade, it is likely that supermarket grocers will continue to recede if they are not able to build more capacity to invest in acquiring and retaining customers. As lopsided as market share is today in favor of national/discount grocers, it will get far more unbalanced in the next few years if the current trajectory is not altered.

I posited earlier what would happen were Amazon to continue to advance its grocery efforts as it broadens its global grocery leadership alongside Walmart. Here's one estimate of where Amazon's U.S. grocery business could be in a decade: $334 billion in sales, or 16 percent market share.

AMAZON'S GROCERY SALES ARE PROJECTED TO CONTINUE ACCELERATING

amazon

WHOLE FOODS

AMAZON'S GROCERY SALES (2003 – 2023 – 2032E)

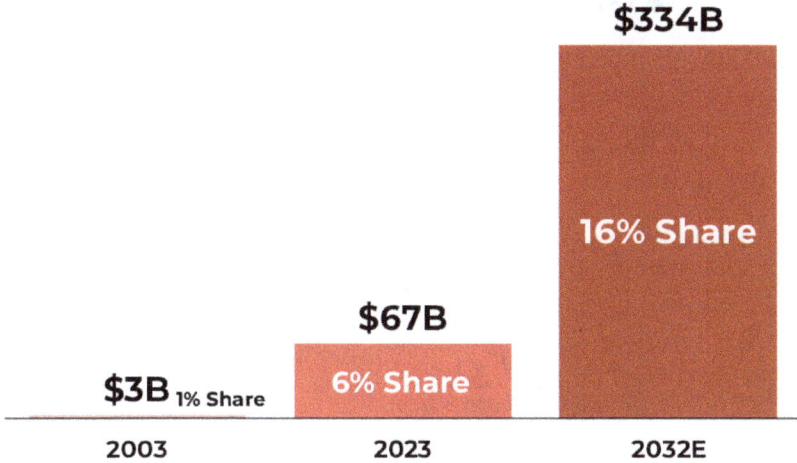

$334B

16% Share

$67B

$3B 1% Share

6% Share

2003   2023   2032E

Source: RS Capital projection.

If we extrapolate the current trend out another 10 years, each of Walmart, Costco and Amazon would make significant market share increases, while supermarket grocers like Kroger, Albertsons and Ahold Delhaize are expected to cede material share.

IN THE NEXT TEN YEARS, NATIONAL / DISCOUNT GROCERS COULD HAVE OVER 75% U.S. GROCERY SHARE

U.S. GROCERY MARKET SHARE – 2023 VS. 2033

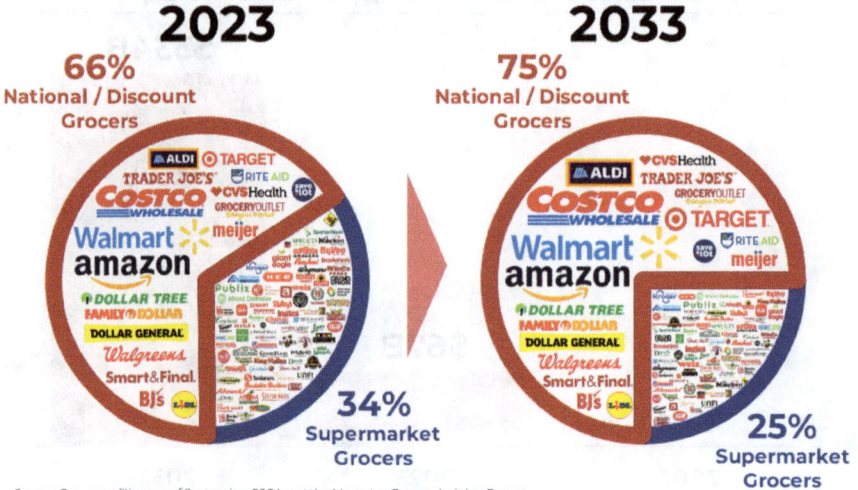

Source: Company filings as of September 2024 and the Mercatus Grocery Insights Report.
Note: U.S. grocery sales excludes pharmacy, fuel and other non-grocery categories. Amazon figures reflect 90% of North America sales (U.S. not reported). Pro forma for Winn Dixie and Harveys stores recently acquired. 2033 market share applies 10-year historical CAGR to each company's current grocery sales (uses 5-year historical CAGR if 10-year unavailable).

In sum, this means that national/discount grocers would control over 75 percent of U.S. grocery.

As a consequence, the Ghost of Supermarkets Future might well show us a story quite similar to that of department stores. It could look something like this:

- Walmart has far more grocery share than all supermarket grocers, *combined*;

- Amazon opens or buys thousands of Amazon Fresh stores and challenges Walmart as the leading grocer globally and in the U.S., meaning *just those two companies* have **nearly 50 percent of U.S. grocery market share**;

- Walmart and Target continue to invest in their wholly-owned delivery infrastructure and much lower prices to retain customers, thereby exacerbating, to a prohibitive degree, the profit challenges of supermarket grocers, whose viability requires reasonably proximate prices to their larger national/discount grocer peers;

- Dollar General expands its leadership as the grocer with the most numerous fresh grocery stores in the U.S., grows its store base from more than 20,000 to over 30,000 (as it has suggested it intends to do over time) and competes with Germany's Aldi to be the leading smaller-box grocer in the country;

- Dozens of supermarket grocery chains, with all the increased competitive pressure, are no longer able to remain profitable and are rationalized away, just like department stores before them;

- Thousands of closed supermarkets pepper America's landscape, their towns having lost part of their foundation and an inextricably connected part of their soul;

- Millions of part-time and full-time supermarket jobs are lost across the country;

- Millions of former supermarket teammates leave grocery or work quasi-robotic shifts in 24/7 Amazon, Walmart and Target fulfillment centers (if their jobs are not automated away by then);

- Consumers have far less grocery choice and far less opportunity for in-store engagement.

THE GHOST OF SUPERMARKETS' FUTURE

In that state of Supermarkets Future, very few supermarket grocers might remain able to provide the bountiful offering and experience Dickens captured over 180 years ago. Remember, Tiny Tim sadly dies in the dystopian future the Spirit shows Scrooge, symbolizing the fate of the smaller, underprivileged have-nots — or, in our parallel case, our beloved and *essential* supermarket grocers.

This version of American grocery's future is simply not acceptable to me, not as a citizen and certainly not as a proud member of this irreplaceable community — this family of service — across the country.

But I am an eternal optimist. I therefore hold out hope for **another version of Supermarkets Future**, another path that each of us has the power to help effect, provided political and other ideological forces don't continue to try to stand in the way.

In this version:

- Thousands of towns across the country still have supermarket grocers continuing to serve as community pillars;

- Various supermarket grocery chains combine to build scale and help create a more reasonable balance of power vis-à-vis the fast-developing national/discount grocer oligarchy;

- Various online, specialty, ethnic, discount and traditional grocers continue to develop and provide consumers more choice, whether stand-alone or as part of larger supermarket grocery organizations;

- More large supermarket grocers with a lower cost of capital become better able to make the sort of technology investments Amazon, Walmart and Target are making in order to retain their close connection and invaluable relationship of trust with their customers;

- Millions of supermarket teammates keep their jobs and continue to have the opportunity to serve customers in a fun and engaging way in their stores, burnishing the brands of their companies every day, strengthening the foundation of their communities and providing limitless opportunity for folks of all ages to start and build great supermarket careers.

This future — a brighter, better grocery sector, as part of a brighter, better America — is worth working for, worth advocating for, every day, until it happens. The question is whether it will be permitted to occur.

U.S. GROCERY STORE LANDSCAPE, CURRENT VS. FUTURE

___

FUTURE

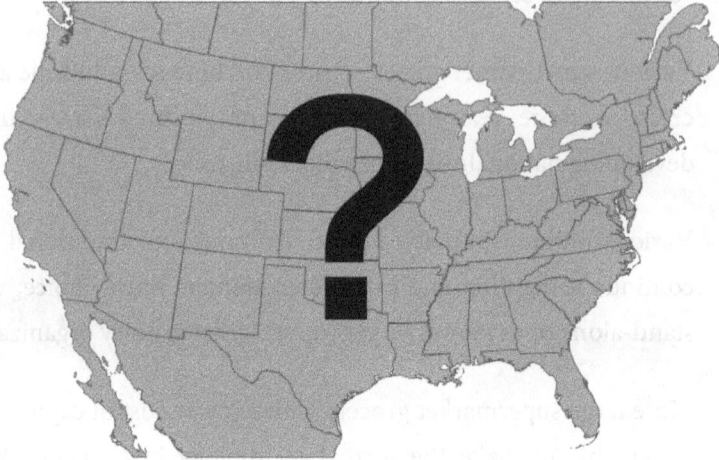

Conclusion

In the preface to *A Christmas Carol*, Dickens wrote that he ***"endeavoured in this Ghostly little book, to raise the Ghost of an Idea, which shall not put my readers out of humour with themselves, with each other, with the season, or with me. May it haunt their houses pleasantly..."***

At the risk of offending many grocery friends and clients, on whose good graces I rely for my livelihood, the Ghost of Supermarkets Future is intended to respectfully spotlight these alternative potential futures for America's supermarket grocers.

By providing members of our wonderful community with empirical perspective, coupled in this case with logical extensions of grocery economics and mathematics, I share here Dickens' earnest and constructive goals in the hope that what I have written will help catalyze the courage to take effective action and the fortitude to see that action through, in order to protect a vulnerable part of America's foundation — which we hold so dear, but which too many take for granted — while it is still possible.

My job as a mergers advisor may be to maximize shareholder value, but I keep score on how many grocery stores and jobs our transactions save or strengthen. It has been thousands of stores and hundreds of thousands of jobs so far. A core part of our mission has always been — and will always be — to help protect these essential grocery jobs and stores from the incessant, extraordinary pressure of the national/discount grocers.

Our supermarket grocers are part of what — to me — is an undeniably better version of America than we would be without them.

As Tiny Tim (who survives in the alternative future Scrooge creates with his transformational actions) offered at the conclusion of the book, best wishes and blessings to *"Every One."*

Remember: *How would you have fed your family?*

Postscript

I wrote most of this book in early July 2024. It was refined over the subsequent few weeks and essentially finalized in September 2024 during dozens of hours of flights going back and forth from New York to Portland, Oregon for the FTC's three-plus week trial challenging the Kroger/Albertsons merger, most of which I attended in person.

I have spent an enormous amount of time over the past two years on Albertsons' behalf trying to educate different constituencies across the country on the realities of American grocery and how much it has changed in the past 20 years. It therefore seemed imperative to spend most of those three weeks there, not only to recognize two years of extremely hard work and earnest dedication by a long list of grocery teammates and advisory partners, but also to bear witness to one of the most pivotal grocery events in our lifetime — in the room where it happened.

The trial was riveting (at least to me) and, in many ways, a solemn experience. I took copious notes so I would be able to make sure the record was clear, at this inflection point that would profoundly impact grocery's strategic landscape for many years, potentially directing which "Supermarkets Future" is in store for America.

A great deal has been written about the trial and decision which I will not attempt to replicate, but I think it important to document a few key testimony takeaways I witnessed, including, as I have been wont to share, a few *"things you might not know."*

The foundation of the FTC's case — literally the very first point it made in its opening statement — purported to address the demonstrably false notion that supermarket grocers have been responsible for post-Covid food inflation; as discussed earlier, this is simply not accurate.

Moreover, there were countless facts presented at trial that were consistent with the points shared in Chapter 7 about the merger, where I enumerate four clear reasons why the proposed transaction was fair, necessary and good for the country, a few of which I summarize below under the same four headings.

#1 — The 2024 grocery market is far more diverse and competitive than the 1980s grocery market the FTC describes.

Kroger's CEO Rodney McMullen noted as he began his testimony that when he started in the industry in the late 1970s, America's #1 grocer was A&P, which, he added, is now gone. He talked about the first time he realized Walmart was a serious competitor, in the late 1980s, when a Kroger store in Dixon, Tennessee, lost 30 percent of its sales after a supercenter opened nearby. Rodney confirmed that Walmart is Kroger's #1 competitor and, as the grocery industry's low-price leader, constantly impacts Kroger's pricing. He confirmed that Costco is Kroger's #2 competitor.

Stuart Aitken, Kroger's chief merchant at the time, said Kroger is *"monomaniacally focused"* on Walmart's pricing (not Albertsons'). He testified that Kroger's prices are highly correlated to Walmart's prices, far more than to any other grocer, and Kroger's prices are no higher versus Walmart in markets where they compete with Albertsons than where they do not.

McMullen testified that the emergence of global companies like Amazon, Costco and Walmart threatened the existence of corner grocery stores. He said that if Albertsons went out of business tomorrow, Kroger could not raise prices without losing customers to those and other competitors.

McMullen also testified that he keeps on his desk a Cincinnati Business Courier newspaper article from 2017 with the headline "How Amazon is Crashing Kroger's Party" (they showed a photo of it on a big screen in the courtroom). Rodney told the court that the clipping is a reminder that Amazon is a "creeping competitor," much like Walmart: *"Every day it reminds me Amazon is going to be a bigger competitor tomorrow than they are today, and we can never forget that."*

This perspective was validated by Amazon's Vice President – Consumables, who testified that Amazon aims to be one of "Earth's most customer-centric companies" with "Earth's broadest consumer selection." (Yes, he said *"Earth's."*) He acknowledged that Amazon has a large and growing grocery business and is working to expand grocery, which is *"intensely competitive…[because] many retailers compete quite fiercely for customers [and] margins are small."*

Vivek Sankaran, Albertsons' CEO, also testified that Walmart sets grocery retail prices. He said *Albertsons customers* spend more at Walmart and as much at Costco as they spend at Albertsons stores. He went on to note that *Albertsons only gets 12 percent of its own customers' "share of wallet,"* meaning 88 percent of Albertsons' customers' grocery sales go to *other grocers*, particularly Walmart (15 percent), Costco (12 percent) and Amazon (6 percent). Additional grocers, including Aldi, Trader Joe's, Target, Sprouts and Grocery Outlet, collectively capture over 50 percent of Albertsons' customers' grocery sales. Only 7 percent goes to Kroger, meaning over 80 percent of Albertsons customers' grocery sales go *not to supermarket grocers*, but mostly to the top global grocers with immense scale advantages. In fact, Walmart sells Kraft macaroni and cheese for less than Albertsons can buy it.

Executives from Walmart, Costco, Amazon, Whole Foods and Target all clearly confirmed in their testimony that they actively compete with Kroger, Albertsons and numerous other grocers for U.S. grocery sales and teammates. They all clearly confirmed that they all offer one-stop grocery shopping to their customers, even though most Americans in 2024 regularly shop at multiple grocers, not just one.

Whole Foods' CMO testified that there is a myriad of grocery choices, and customers shop at four to seven different grocers. Costco's SVP of Food & Sundries testified that Costco offers better value for customers than supermarket grocers, which have difficulty competing on price. Target's SVP of Merchandising – Food & Beverage talked about how much Target's grocery business has recently grown and Target's strong commitment to continuing that growth. Walmart's VP of Merchandising Operations discussed how Walmart's "Every Day Low Price" ("EDLP") strategy is core to the company's philosophy and culture and stated plainly that Walmart's low-price strategy would not be affected by the Kroger/Albertsons merger.

Notably, in the area immediately around the Portland federal courthouse, there are over 20 grocers serving consumers, most of which deliver: Walmart has several stores in the vicinity (that all deliver); Amazon Fresh, Whole Foods and Amazon Prime (that all deliver); four WinCo stores (that all deliver); Trader Joe's; plus over a dozen different Instacart grocery delivery choices, including Costco, Target, 99 Ranch, Grocery Outlet, New Seasons, Natural Grocers, CVS, Walgreens, Rite Aid, Chefs Store, Restaurant Depot and Jackson's Food Stores, along with Kroger- and Albertsons-owned banners.

The FTC excluded most of these grocers from the "supermarkets market" it put forth.

The FTC also suggested supermarket grocers don't compete with various national/discount and specialty grocers because of various differences in their stores, including concrete floors (which many supermarket grocers have), higher ceilings and the type of bananas they sell, e.g., organic, fair trade or otherwise (no, I'm not kidding).

#2 — Kroger has a long track record of better prices and better wages and made clear commitments to improve prices and wages even more with the Albertsons acquisition.

Kroger's McMullen was explicitly clear in his testimony: ***"The day that we merge is the day that we will begin lowering prices,"*** as he reiterated the company's commitment to lower prices for customers by $1 billion per year. As evidence of Kroger's ability to deliver on this promise, McMullen discussed the company's long track record of investing in lower prices over the past 20 years.

Kroger's Aitken testified that Albertsons prices are ~10 to 12 percent higher than Kroger, which manifested both the necessity and the opportunity to bring prices down at Albertsons' stores.

Kroger also presented an exceptionally detailed plan — consistent with its extensive successful experience delivering on price investments in previous acquisitions — to capture cost savings and other efficiencies to help pay for price, wage and store investments at Albertsons. The plan included savings in the cost of national brand, private label and fresh groceries, pharmacy, goods not for resale, supply chain, technology and administrative overhead.

The FTC tried to undermine parts of this plan by suggesting they do not "count" in the FTC's 2023 Merger Guidelines (which seem intentionally designed to exclude many transaction cost savings and make efficiencies more difficult for merging parties to validate), notwithstanding the fact that in the real world, these would be real cash savings that would give Kroger a real ability to make these investments to help them better compete with Walmart, Costco, Amazon, Aldi and others.

Aitken was crystal clear on his expectations that Kroger would meet its commitments to its customers, team and the market: *"I know it."*

#3 — The grocery labor market is very fluid; it's not a rigid, monolithic group of unionized supermarket workers.

The FTC put forth an unprecedented theory that there's a discrete labor market for unionized supermarket workers in order to challenge the merger.

As it turns out, testimony demonstrated that over 98 percent of Kroger and Albertsons employees come from other employers such as non-union grocers like Walmart, Target, Costco or Amazon, or other employers like Starbucks, UPS, FedEx, Home Depot, Foot Locker, Macy's, Subway and McDonald's. When employees leave Kroger or Albertsons, over 99 percent go to such other employers, meaning only one or two percent of Kroger and Albertsons employees come from or go to the other.

It therefore seems difficult to suggest that there is a specialized market for unionized supermarket workers, notwithstanding the fact that America's grocers and grocery workers have proven themselves to be essential and indefatigable when we need them most.

#4 — C&S would become a leading grocery retailer, poised to maintain competition across divestiture markets.

Yael Cosset, Kroger's SVP and CIO, described Kroger's three key requirements for the divestiture buyer: (1) strategic commitment to the business; (2) direct and indirect experience; and (3) financial wherewithal to be a successful competitor.

C&S' CEO Eric Winn discussed C&S' grocery heritage and its supply scale across the country, as well as the many services it provides to retail customers and franchisees that are similar to those which a larger grocer centrally provides to its owned stores, including merchandising assortment, category management, store design and construction, store technology, print media, digital marketing and data insights. He talked through C&S' broader strategy to expand its retail footprint, after years of focusing more on its supply business. Winn testified that *"...we are going to compete very aggressively from day one. We have to, to be successful....We owe it to our people. We owe it to the consumers. We owe it to ourselves to compete strongly. And if we don't do that, we won't be successful."*

Asked if he could assure the Court and the FTC that C&S intends to operate the stores, Winn definitively answered, *"Absolutely. We have to. In order to be a successful business, we have to."*

Winn also discussed C&S' plans to invest over $1 billion in lower prices and capital improvements. While this would lower EBITDA in the near term (as price investments usually do), C&S expected to generate several billion dollars in cumulative cash flow from the acquisition, which would not only improve its legacy supply business but also be well more than required to finance those investments. Winn added that $900 million of the $2.9 billion purchase price — over 30 percent of the cost — would be paid in equity from the Cohen family ($500 million) and from SoftBank ($400 million), its massive, global investment partner with over $100 billion in assets under management. (This is far more equity capital, it was later testified, than the roughly 10 percent that was invested in Haggen's over-leveraged acquisition of divested stores a decade earlier.) With respect to the important commitment the Cohen family was making to the success of this investment, Winn said, *"[O]ne of the reasons why I feel so fortunate and proud to be a member of this company and to work for the Cohen family is their commitment to the business in the next 106 years."*[61]

Susan Morris, Albertsons' outstanding COO, who was tapped to be the CEO of the divestiture retail grocery business C&S was to acquire, has been with Albertsons for 35 years and helped build the company from 200 stores to its current 2,300 stores. As COO, she currently oversees nearly 500 of the 579 stores C&S agreed to buy. She testified that she is *"confident in our ability to run these stores"* and said that C&S' principal owner, Rick Cohen, gave her a clear assurance that C&S intended to run the business for the long term. Various executives testified they were confident in C&S' ability to be successful and / or were excited to join C&S because of Susan.

The FTC argued that rebannered stores would not be successful ongoing competitors because of challenges experienced by C&S and other buyers in previous acquisitions. In response, Morris told the court that she has extensive experience with successful store banner changes, including when Albertsons acquired American Stores in 1998 and following its A&P and Safeway acquisitions in 2015. She noted various key differences with this acquisition and past challenges, including C&S' supply chain strength; the extended three-year time period that would be afforded to re-banner stores (versus an immediate conversion requirement in past transactions); the comprehensive tech systems platform C&S was buying (a clone of the Albertsons tech stack, on which most of the divestiture stores already run); and the 67,000 store-level and 1,000 corporate teammates who planned to join her to operate the business, with C&S' support.

---

[61] I attended the examinations of each of the witnesses discussed here, and many others, but I was not present when Eric Winn testified in Portland. I did watch Winn's Washington and Colorado trial examinations remotely (on the courts' livestreams) and reviewed the transcript of his Portland testimony (which was consistent with his testimony in the state trials), from which this material is sourced.

Morris talked extensively about her plans for rejuvenating the stores and her excitement about the team joining her in the mission: ***"These are my people. This is where I've spent my life. I'm very qualified to do this."***

FTC's Cherry-Picked Emails and Texts

The FTC "cherry-picked" various emails and texts following the merger announcement (many visceral reactions to the news and others selectively out of context) in an apparent attempt to exaggerate the extent to which the two companies compete with each other, to challenge Kroger's lower-price and higher-wage commitments and to discredit C&S as a buyer of the divestiture business. None of these texts or emails was a Board presentation or official company strategy. None of these texts or emails changed the economic facts of the extreme size and strength of the global grocers that control over two-thirds of American grocery in 2024 (and growing). None of these texts or emails changed Kroger's laser focus on Walmart for pricing; Kroger's official business plan of investing in better prices and its track record of doing so for nearly 20 years; that the overwhelming majority of Kroger and Albertsons customers' grocery sales go to <u>other grocers</u> (not to Albertsons); or C&S' scale and capabilities.

Not surprisingly, the FTC ignored thousands of exculpatory emails and texts from Kroger and Albertsons executives that focused on their many other grocery competitors, particularly Walmart, Costco, Amazon, Aldi, Target, Dollar General and various specialty/ethnic grocers.

The FTC also argued that C&S was not qualified because there were communications conceding the possibility that an acquired store might need to be closed at some point in the future. This was frustrating to hear because as any grocer knows, no supermarket grocer could responsibly commit to being able to indefinitely withstand the extraordinary, relentless competitive pressures from the national/discount grocers that have roughly doubled their

U.S. grocery market share in the past 20 years. It would simply be indefensible for any supermarket grocer to suggest it could be perpetually immune to these pressures and would never have an unprofitable store.

FTC's Hypothetical Competition Analysis

The FTC called as a witness an economist to evaluate the potential anticompetitive impact of the merger. The FTC's economist presented a "hypothetical monopolist" analysis that suggested the combination could *theoretically* cause upward pricing pressure in certain markets that *might* lead to an increase in prices, notwithstanding Kroger's lower price track record, its repeated commitments to immediately lower prices upon closing the transaction, and the planned C&S divestiture to preserve competition.

The FTC economist simply defined these markets with circles around a store, disregarding evidence about where people *actually* shop. For example, these circles did not account for shopping patterns impacted by rivers, bridges, neighboring towns or the fact that many national/discount grocers like Walmart and Costco draw customers from a much wider radius than supermarket grocers; though their stores might sit just outside a five-mile radius circle, they draw customers from 10 or 15 miles away (as was corroborated by various industry witnesses and acknowledged by the economist on cross examination), i.e., they should be included in the "market."

The FTC's economist chose not to incorporate into his model the combined effect of the extensive group of grocers who *actually* compete with Kroger and Albertsons (Costco, Sam's, Whole Foods, Aldi, Trader Joe's, Sprouts, Dollar General, Family Dollar, Hmart, 99 Ranch, Northgate, Cardenas, etc.), Kroger's planned price investments and the offsetting impact of C&S operating divestiture stores as a competitor. Kroger's economist argued this would have brought the anti-competitive store count to zero.

These analyses are very sensitive to the inputs that comprise them; ultimately, as Rodney McMullen testified — and common sense in 2024 American grocery confirms — *you simply cannot raise prices while Walmart, Costco, Amazon and Aldi lower prices and then hope to retain your customers.*

A Gift to Walmart and Costco and Other Global Grocers

Vivek Sankaran testified that blocking the merger would be a huge loss to communities and would be *"a gift"* to Walmart, Costco and other larger grocery competitors.

FTC Chair Scapegoats Grocers on *60 Minutes*

Just after arguments in Portland concluded in mid-September 2024, FTC Chair Lina Khan appeared on *60 Minutes* and continued to scapegoat grocers for food inflation in order to justify the FTC's case. This felt like an unfair and inappropriate use of a national megaphone at a sensitive time in the trial; post-trial briefs were about to be filed, and the judge was presumably just beginning to deliberate her decision. (Khan did this in between campaign stops for various politicians, which was also unexpected for the head of a supposedly independent, non-partisan government agency.)

Washington and Colorado Trials

Because Washington and Colorado did not join the FTC's case like various other states, after the FTC's trial in Oregon federal court ended, the companies had to repeat the exercise in successive state trials in Washington and Colorado. In Washington, the attorney general, who was running for governor (and won), campaigned extensively on his efforts to help prevent the merger, trumpeting the same questionable arguments as the FTC. The states' AGs and their counsel were able to watch the FTC trial in preparation for their own.

It was also grueling on a human level for the companies' legal teams, who were essentially away from their families for over two months. I likened them to boxers, enduring one long fight while their next opponent casually watched, then a second long fight while the third opponent watched and then finally taking on the third opponent. From my perspective, one never would have known the companies' legal teams were battling three consecutive trials; they handled themselves with complete professionalism throughout.

I could write several more chapters describing hundreds of nuances that were testified, challenged and rebutted, but 12 weeks after closing arguments in Portland, we had a decision.

Federal Court Decision

On December 10, 2024, Judge Adrienne Nelson of the U.S. District Court for the District of Oregon granted a preliminary injunction to block the transaction. Roughly an hour later, Judge Marshall Ferguson in Washington state court did the same. I will focus on Judge Nelson's opinion as the two opinions are similar.

In short, Judge Nelson rejected the extensive evidence the companies presented about the broad competitive nature of American grocery shopping in 2024 and concluded that supermarkets are a submarket that should be the basis of competitive analysis, mainly because, she suggested, they comprise a unique source of a one-stop shopping for groceries:

> *Supermarkets are distinct from other grocery retailers. Supermarkets offer a larger selection of fresh and non-perishable items, a one-stop shopping experience that appeals to a particular consumer's preference to meet all their grocery needs in one location, and a customer service focus with deli, bakery, meat, and other specialized departments. The evidence that industry professionals understand supermarkets to be a*

distinct category of stores that compete with each other, and that supermarkets monitor each other's pricing and are sensitive to changes, bolsters the conclusion that supermarkets are a submarket within grocery retailers.

This reasoning rejected the evidence presented that various national/ discount, specialty / ethnic and other grocers also offer a one-stop shop and compete with supermarket grocers in their efforts to do so. It ignored the fact that online grocery is the means by which millions of Americans shop for groceries, whether at one grocer or several. It disregarded the fact that supermarket grocers also monitor many other grocers' prices as well.

Judge Nelson distinguished Costco, Aldi, Whole Foods, Amazon, dollar grocers and ethnic grocers from supermarket grocers; she dismissed both the importance of Walmart as a competitor and the companies' extensive focus on Walmart grocery pricing, writing:

The overarching goals of antitrust law are not met...by permitting an otherwise unlawful merger in order to permit firms to compete with an industry giant.

Judge Nelson also rejected Kroger's promises to invest billions in better prices, higher wages and better stores:

The promise to make a price investment is not legally binding, and the court must give limited weight to a non-binding promise made during these proceedings.

The FTC's novel labor market theory was not successful, though the judge did tentatively suggest the *"relatively unusual market definition"* could be plausible. She ultimately concluded that there was not sufficient economic analysis presented to verify the claim.

Finally, Judge Nelson rejected the divestiture to C&S as a sufficient remedy to "negate any anticompetitive effects of the merger." She focused less on C&S' strengths as a leading grocery wholesaler for the past 100 years and the quality of the pro forma company and more on concerns about C&S' size relative to Albertsons, its potential reliance on Kroger from their Transition Services Agreement (TSA), and challenges C&S experienced with past grocery store acquisitions. C&S was clear that its prior acquisitions were intended to keep struggling customer stores in business and preserve grocery supply, unlike this transaction's attempt at broad strategic transformation by acquiring a strong multi-regional retail operation; the judge did not accept this distinction:

> *There is ample evidence that the divestiture is not sufficient in scale to adequately compete with the merged firm and is structured in a way that will significantly disadvantage C&S as a competitor. C&S' history of unsuccessful grocery store ventures and its continuing dependence on defendants throughout the TSA period also suggest that the divestiture will not adequately restore competition....The deficiencies in the divestiture scope and structure create a risk that some or all of the divested stores will lose sales or close, as has happened in past C&S acquisitions.*

Ironically, just hours after the decision, Andrew Ferguson was nominated by the President-elect to be the new Chair of the FTC, replacing Lina Khan.

The next day, however, Albertsons terminated the merger agreement and sued Kroger for breach of contract. As of this writing, it is not clear how that dispute will be resolved.

The "Political" Ghost of Supermarkets Future

Justice Louis Brandeis once wrote *"sunlight is the best disinfectant."* Unfortunately, we live in a time where politicians and their agents routinely transform facts and obfuscate the truth to fit a narrative that is politically expedient. The debate about Kroger/Albertsons became nakedly political at precisely the worst time, ahead of a presidential election.

I had hoped that the "sunlight" of incontrovertible grocery facts and the earnest and oft-repeated public commitments from trusted leaders like Rodney McMullen, Vivek Sankaran, Eric Winn and Susan Morris would have disinfected the FTC's gross mischaracterizations amid the storm of misdirected political winds gusting behind them. It seems I was wrong.

Irrespective of your politics — whatever you think about tax policy, social issues, climate change or America's place in the world — the politicization of our industry is awful and, in many cases, just plain ignorant.

In the wake of this decision, numerous politicians are celebrating the result, usurping credit for preventing a transaction that they disingenuously claim would have raised grocery prices, even though the facts clearly suggest it would have lowered prices, raised wages and strengthened the stores' ability to compete with national/discount grocers. I suspect many of those with the loudest voices, those spouting the most preposterous talking points, could not answer basic questions about the history, operations or economics of our industry.

★ ★ ★ ★

Some people seem to think that our supermarket grocers operate on some island, insulated from Walmart, Costco and Amazon, the same global forces that disrupted and destabilized department stores — they do not.

In 2024, it is plainly evident in the vast majority of markets that supermarket grocers primarily compete not with each other, but with these (and other) national / discount grocers. The willfully blind, gerrymandered view to the contrary is highly misleading and irresponsibly impedes supermarket grocers' ability to build the scale required to remain vibrant in the long run for customers, teammates and communities.

If we're not careful, we will lose many of them, and many people will wish they'd have contributed more informed and balanced perspective during this sensitive time.

It doesn't have to be this way. *"Sunlight"* and stoic determination can still deliver the right path for Supermarkets Future.

I remain steadfast in my commitment to continue to do everything possible to help protect our supermarket grocers, their teams and their communities.

We have a lot of work to do — let's get to it.

Scott Moses
December 2024

Acknowledgements

I love supermarkets. We are so lucky as consumers to have them in our communities, and I am so lucky that I have been able to inhabit a "corner of the sky" in our indispensable grocery industry, with countless friends, colleagues and clients across the country who have been so warm and welcoming over the past 20-plus years. I am still very much inspired to continue my service in the critically important mission to protect our local supermarket grocers for generations to come.

Mergers advisory work is not singles tennis; it's a team sport. And my team is spectacular.

You have seen throughout this book a dashboard of analyses, charts, maps and other graphics that help us stay on top of countless grocery trends and new developments, from what's happening in the grocery world on a macro basis to the micro perspective and its implications on our clients and their peers.

To make sense of continuously shifting dynamics and confidently advise our clients with conviction and nuanced perspective requires indefatigable commitment to perfection in our work product. It requires rigorous focus on the math and other facets of the strategic calculus that dictates the optimal strategic path. It requires tactical excellence in our execution, all while being truly good, warm people who are consistently collaborative as constructive members of our clients' teams.

It simply would not be possible for me to lead our clients well through their transactions — and not possible for us to have achieved dozens of exceptional outcomes for our clients and their owners — without the extraordinary members of my team, past and present. Like our grocery clients and friends around the country, they too answer the bell each morning to serve, devoted to our quest of protecting supermarket grocers, their stores, their teammates and their communities. Our work is undeniably important, and I am admittedly demanding, continuously processing, chiseling and refining our material to make sure we are always putting forth our very best, leaving it all on the field — every day — for our clients and for the better version of Supermarkets Future.

I particularly want to thank Josh Heft, who has been my right-hand lieutenant for over five years, as well as Greg Grambling for over 10 years before Josh. I also want to thank Victor Farr, Shea Kutner, Eric Yan, Rex Tavello and Joanna Levy, all of whom have also helped me advise clients on multiple transactions and create many of the charts in this book. I want to acknowledge all of our exceptional analysts, Chris James, Garret Goodman, Reedy Clark, Eunice Ra, Armon Lotfi, Colton Moraine and particularly Niraj Komatineni, who has been instrumental in working with me (with the help of some outstanding interns) to optimize and update the dozens of charts in this book. While we've had so many fantastic teammates over the years, Diya Talwar, Andrew Schwartz, Kyle Schlotman, Ben Phillips and Sebastian Sinisterra all made significant contributions to our practice and remain good friends, in some cases after over 20 years. They have all represented the very best of the M&A advisory industry.

My assistant Grace Huh has always been dependable, moving mountains to help me crisscross the country for clients and still get home on time. Kalen Holliday has been very helpful in navigating the publishing element of this book.

Our former senior advisors, Justin Dye (Grocery) and Edna Morris (Restaurants), have spectacular knowledge and experience, but they are even better people. They have been great partners to me over the years.

Justin and I met in 2005 when he helped lead the original acquisition by Cerberus of the 661 "non-core" Albertsons stores that were eventually turned around to be the foundation for a series of acquisitions and improvements that became the company we know today. He was CSO and then COO at Albertsons, spanning a decade, and remains the single grocery executive to whom we've sold the most of our clients' companies. We developed such a strong relationship of trust over those transactions that after he left Albertsons, we teamed up and did some great work together.

Peter J. Solomon, the founder of our firm, Solomon Partners (formerly known as Peter J. Solomon Company and PJ Solomon), is the scion of two great retail families. Peter's father was Chairman and CEO of Abraham & Straus; his mother's family owned Stop & Shop. The most prestigious award one can receive from FMI is the Sidney Rabb award, named for Peter's uncle, his mother's brother. Peter has been one of the great retail M&A advisors for over 60 years, a lion of investment banking. Since we met over eight years ago, Peter — who is in his mid-80s — has been a dear friend and venerated mentor. A few hours before the Kroger-Albertsons decision was handed down, Peter shared with me an op-ed he wrote in *The Washington Post* just over 20 years ago, which was truly prophetic:

"The FTC needs to update its historical, now largely anachronistic definition of 'markets' to reflect more accurately Walmart's dominant position and allow others to join forces to compete."[62]

---

[62] https://www.washingtonpost.com/archive/opinions/2004/03/28/a-lesson-from-wal-mart/fdded422-6da7-4457-a849-854d482f78b6/

Like all great advisors, Peter teaches me something in every conversation we have. I hope to continue to live up to and honor the prodigious example he has set.

Marc Cooper, our CEO at Solomon Partners, has been a dear friend and supporter of our practice. Our firm has more than doubled in size since I joined in 2016; Marc's long-term vision for our firm and the optimistic tenacity with which he has led our partnership in its pursuit have been spectacular to witness.

My partners at Solomon are remarkable. From retail to consumer, media, out-of-home advertising, infrastructure, power & renewables, financial services, healthcare, business services, industrials, distribution, technology and more (as we grow), their exceptional service and consistently spectacular results for numerous companies, private equity firms and lenders have been marvelous, particularly as we have built our firm into one of the leading independent financial advisory firms in the United States (and beyond).

In the fall of 1999, Pete Martelli and I were officemates, working nights part-time at Simpson Thacher, trying to put ourselves through law school. As we regularly plugged away late into the night before classes the next morning, we often talked about the commitment and sacrifices we knew we would need to make to even have a chance of building a productive career in M&A (let alone a robust practice). Later that year, I decided to get an MBA to facilitate the path to M&A investment banking advisory work; Pete went on to become one of the top M&A attorneys in the country (now at Kirkland) and one of my closest friends. I will always be grateful for his helpful perspective over the years; it's amazing how powerful and enduring the right words of friendship can be at pivotal moments.

* * *

I noted at the very beginning of this book the extraordinary experience I had with my first grocery friends at Pathmark. I have been so incredibly fortunate to have made so many wonderful friends in our industry in the 20-plus years since that first transaction.

Jim Donald, in particular, has been an invaluable mentor and dear friend. Jim showed me how to lead and manage a team at a very early and impressionable point in my career. I am so lucky he has shared such astute perspective on our industry and has been such a great partner, including when working together for the Haggen family and for Albertsons. Jim is in his 70s now and could probably still take me in one-on-one basketball (though I like my chances in conference room H-O-R-S-E).

Mike Schlotman, Kroger's inimitable CFO for 20 years through 2019, has been a phenomenal mentor. He and his wonderful wife Teri are two of the very best people I know and have been dear friends of ours for many years. Mike was an exceptional partner on various engagements we executed for Kroger, including when we advised the company on its acquisition of Roundy's in 2015. His unique, down-to-earth personality — even as a financial guy (and he is a brilliant one) — made working with him so special. At a pivotal moment in my life, Mike provided some of the most meaningful, eye-opening and motivating advice I've ever received, catalyzing the development of this practice, for which I will always be deeply indebted to him.

Jim and Mike both had humble beginnings and remain humble to this day. (I like to think we have that in common; it is certainly one reason why I've always admired them.) They are constant reminders that it's not where you start that matters, but who you are when you get to your destination. Their remarkable talent, coupled with true family-oriented leadership, makes them not just incredibly well-respected, but deeply appreciated by everyone around them.

There have been so many other exceptional leaders who have been extremely generous in allowing me a window into the example of excellence they set managing their companies and teams, and/or sharing valuable viewpoints about our industry and its constant evolution: Rodney McMullen, Vivek Sankaran, Bob Miller, Len Tessler, Scott Wille, Lisa Gray, Mark Gross, Frank Vitrano, Neil Golub, Jerry Golub, Bob Schwartz, Scott Grimmett, Jack Stahl, Lou Giraudo, Chris McGarry, Kenneth McGrath, Salah Nafal, Mario Nafal, Stew Leonard, Jr., Suzy Monford, Kevin Barner, Michael Needler, Brian Carney, Judy Spires, Sylvain Perrier, Chieh Huang, Tres Lund, Melissa Ben-Ishay, Abel Porter, Rob Bartels, Brad Brookshire, John Franklin, Randall Onstead, John Clougher, Ken Nemeth, Joe DiDomizio, John Catsimatidis, Tim Kelleher, Chris Sherrell, Or Raitses, Jean Coutu, Francios Coutu, Alice Elliot, Leslie Sarasin, Mark Baum, Dagmar Farr, Tom Furphy, Kevin Coupe, Rob Woseth, Tom O'Boyle, Bo Sharon, Robert Taylor, SuzAnn Kirby, Mike Provenzano (and sons), Andy Jhawar, Kevin Easler, Shon Boney and Doug Sanders, among many, many others.

Doug and I recently partnered working on KKR's sale of Cardenas (Doug was CEO) to Heritage Grocers (owned by Apollo), but we met nearly 20 years ago when he was a rising leader (and eventually a very successful CEO) at Sprouts, working together for Sprouts' co-founder and first CEO, Shon Boney. Shon was not only one of the kindest, most fun, most talented grocers I've known, but he was a wonderful family man and the first grocery CEO to hire our team as we were on the precipice of creating a bona fide independent grocery advisory practice.

Shon and I had countless conversations as we navigated the growth of his business (which had roughly 10 stores when we first met), leading to the mergers we helped execute between Sprouts and both Henry's and Sunflower in 2011 and 2012, respectively, that became the Sprouts which he, Doug and Andy Jhawar at Apollo took public in 2013 with spectacular success. Shon remained humble and generous after the IPO, unassumingly volunteering his time and plane to fly veterans and other people who needed help getting medical care. Shon and I were friends until we lost him in 2021 — way too young.

I think of Shon often. I hope he knew how much I appreciated him, not only for what he helped cultivate in me, but more importantly for the example he set showing all of us the very best of our kind and generous grocery family.

Bob Piccinini, Mike DeFabis, Don Haggen, Tim King and Ken Mueller also left indelible marks on the industry broadly and me personally before leaving us too soon.

* * *

My grandfather once told me that whatever you put in is what you take out. I have tried to live by that sage advice and pass it on.

I am grateful to my parents for the sacrifices they made to put me in a position to have the opportunity to make something of myself. They introduced me to retail by frequently talking about different operators over the dinner table, as they had a small business that was a supplier to department stores. We directly suffered the impact of the changes in that industry as I was coming of age. That experience never left us — it reverberates to this day. It also formed the basis of my central thesis for the grocery industry.

I will always appreciate my big brother David, who charted the path for me from a very young age and has since been an unyielding source of strength amid the inevitable challenges of life. My niece and nephew are lucky to have him in their lives, as am I.

To my in-laws, Andrea and Ira: As we've become close over the years, I see more and more of you both in Jessica's extraordinary qualities. You have treated me like a son for nearly 30 years. I am forever in your debt for your friendship and support, and for raising Jessica to be so delightfully different than anyone else I've ever known.

Finally, to the two loves of my life, my magnificent, brilliant, beautiful and talented wife, Jessica, and our incomparable (and equally magnificent, brilliant, beautiful and talented) daughter, Gabi:

Jessica has been my friend for over 40 years. We met in first grade, where she was the smartest girl by far (I was not the smartest boy). We were often in the same classes growing up and performed together on stage multiple times. We started dating toward the end of college and have been together ever since. When I got my first paycheck after grad school, I had $5.35 in the bank, whatever was in my pocket and a six-figure educational debt that at the time seemed insurmountable. Jessica looked beyond these hurdles in my path and stuck with me through what became an Odyssean journey. After graduating *Phi Beta Kappa* from Princeton and then Yale Law School, she became an incredibly successful litigator and long-time partner at a large international law firm. She has endured my countless trips away and team or client calls disrupting dinners, vacations and family time. She has let herself be coaxed into joining me on scores of supermarket visits over the years (including a Safeway on our honeymoon). She has understood the stresses of my job from my early days as a young banker (my second day on the job after training was September 11, 2001, which essentially shut down M&A for two years) to the ongoing pressures of excellence, leadership and results for our clients as our grocery advisory business has grown. She is a spectacular mother and has set an impeccable example for Gabi in masterfully balancing the various facets of life, both personal and professional. In short, I have been trying to be worthy of her for many, many years. I will keep trying.

Gabi is the light of our world. She has been walking supermarkets with me since she could walk and has been equally patient with the demands of my job. We've had countless conversations in stores and restaurants about gross profit, rent and store expenses — more than any kid should have to tolerate, but she has. Gabi's annual charity lemonade stands, from age four until age nine (before Covid hit) were legendary, with a bunch of great grocery lessons plainly evident: superior product (freshly-cut lemon in each glass), great value (free homemade cookie with each glass), strong local advertising sponsorship (yes, we sold advertising for a lemonade stand), good ambience and family-oriented service — leading to thousands of dollars of donations. There was a P&L, expense management and a summary spreadsheet; she may be a grocer yet....But most important, Gabi is a good, kind, caring, gritty and accomplished girl, who does the work every day to build her strong foundation and embody her name. She knows that goodness is more important than greatness. For all that and so much more, I am immeasurably proud of her.

I love you both beyond words. You give meaning and purpose to everything I do. I simply could not have done any of it without you.

About the Author

Scott Moses is a Partner and Head of Grocery, Pharmacy and Restaurants Investment Banking at Solomon Partners, and a member of the Firm's Operating Committee. He focuses on grocery mergers, acquisitions, sales and divestitures. Scott has advised clients in some of the most significant grocery M&A transactions over the past two decades, with a combined transaction value of over $50 billion. Scott was named to the "Top 50: Americas M&A Dealmakers" list by Global M&A Network (2013) and "40 Under 40" lists of promising finance professionals by IDD (2011) and The M&A Advisor (2015).

Scott's numerous clients (many family-owned), have included Kroger, Albertsons, Sprouts Farmers Market, Sunflower Farmers Market, New Seasons, Roche Bros., Cardenas Markets (KKR), El Rancho, Mi Pueblo, Pro's Ranch Markets, Fresh Encounter, FreshDirect, Mercatus, Boxed, Imperfect Foods, Baked By Melissa, Price Chopper/Market 32, Save Mart, Southeastern Grocers, Save A Lot, United Supermarkets, Fairway, Kings/Balducci's, Lucky's Market, Best Market, Martin's, Haggen, Lund's/Byerly's, Supervalu (Shop & Save), Central Grocers, Marsh, Rite Aid (Lenders), Jean Coutu (Brooks/Eckerd), Fred's (Rx) and Weis Markets (SuperPetz), as well as many private equity firms.

Scott has appeared on and/or been quoted as a sector thought leader numerous times in various business and grocery media outlets, including Bloomberg, CNN, Forbes, Fox Business, Reuters, The Wall Street Journal, The

Washington Post, Yahoo Finance, Food Dive, Food Institute, Morning News Beat, Progressive Grocer, Shelby Report, Supermarket News and Winsight Grocery. He writes a quarterly column in Supermarket News and has been a frequent speaker over many years at conferences for FMI, GroceryShop, NGA and several other organizations.

Scott was previously the Head of Food, Drug and Specialty Retail Investment Banking at Sagent Advisors, prior to which he worked in the retail investment banking groups at JPMorgan, Citigroup and Dresdner Kleinwort Wasserstein (Wasserstein Perella).

Scott graduated *summa cum laude* with a BA in Political Science from the University of Pennsylvania and received a JD/MBA from Columbia University, where he was a Harlan Fiske Stone Scholar and an executive editor of the Columbia Business Law Review.

Scott sits on the Board of Directors of UpLift Solutions, a national nonprofit originally founded to bring full-service grocery stores to food deserts. He is also a Fellow of the Culinary Institute of America.

Scott lives in New York City and Connecticut with his wife and daughter, both of whom became exceptional amateur chefs during Covid.